THE CHANGING FACE OF ISLAM IN AMERICA

The Changing Face of Islam in America

Understanding and Reaching Your Muslim Neighbor

Larry A. Poston

with
Carl F. Ellis, Jr.

HORIZON BOOKS

CAMP HILL, PENNSYLVANIA

HORIZON BOOKs

a division of Christian Publications, Inc.
3825 Hartzdale Drive
Camp Hill, PA 17011
www.cpi-horizon.com

The Changing Face
of Islam in America
ISBN: 0-88965-168-X
LOC Catalog Card Number: 99-080157

Contents

Introduction

While teaching at Greater Europe Mission's Nordic Bible Institute in the early 1980s, my wife and I came in contact with several Middle Eastern families who were applying for political asylum in Sweden. The Swedish government had relocated them to our town, and only a narrow courtyard separated our dwellings. They came from several different countries, but they all had one thing in common: they were Muslims. We found we could befriend some of these families quite easily. In fact, many of them were far more comfortable speaking English than attempting to learn the language of a country which might or might not be their future home.

One young Lebanese man took particular delight in conversing with me, perhaps because I had been able to guess the engine size of a Pontiac TransAm he showed me in a photograph. The car had been his pride and joy before it was blown to pieces—

along with his home—during the bombing in Beirut in 1983. I was surprised that he would want to befriend an American, since many Lebanese blamed the United States for their suffering during those years. But such was not the case with my friend; he was as angry as any American would be over the suicide bombing of the Marine barracks. He considered this act a disgrace to his country and a defilement of his religion.

All of the families we met were winsome, and our relationships with them were cordial and relaxed. They invited us to coffee and laughed at the antics of our infant daughter. We played with their children and spent most of our time discussing politics and religion—the two subjects which good etiquette says to avoid at all costs! But while we disagreed about Islam as a means of relating to God, the discussions never became heated. We always parted on good terms. There was never an attempt on their part to denounce my faith in Christ, nor did they ever seek to convince my wife or me to convert to their religious beliefs.

Perhaps this demeanor came from their desire to leave the best impression while awaiting a decision on their visas, or perhaps it came from a general passiveness regarding their Islamic beliefs—I don't know. But partly because of these highly positive experiences, I made the decision to concentrate upon Islam in my doctoral studies.

Taking Up the Gauntlet

My first encounter with *activist* Muslims, however, was one of the most humiliating experiences of my life. I was beginning field research for my dissertation and had made contact with the Islamic Information Center of America, a Muslim organization located in suburban Chicago. I had an appointment to meet the director, who was greatly interested in my project and had promised to help however he could.

When I arrived for what I thought would be a private meeting, I found four additional Muslim men present. After a few minutes of introductions, one of the guests said, "Musa says that you are a Christian." I had told my host this during an earlier telephone conversation, and so I responded that it was indeed correct. The man smiled. "Good. Would you mind if I asked you some questions?" he asked. Even though the purpose of my visit was to ask questions of them, I said that I would not mind at all.

As a graduate of a conservative Midwestern Bible college and a well-known evangelical seminary, and with a term of missionary experience behind me, I was somewhat confident. When the man asked if I would explain something in John 1, I expected a discussion on the opening verses which identify the Word of God—i.e., Jesus—with God Himself. But much to my surprise, he asked me to begin reading in verse 19. "Now this was John's testimony when the Jews of Jerusalem sent priests and Levites to ask him who he was. He did not fail to confess, but confessed freely, 'I am not the Christ' " (1:19-20).

"Stop right there a minute," said my Muslim questioner. "It appears that the Jews were expecting certain important people to appear among them, is that not so? Here it tells of their expectation that the Christ would come, is that correct?"

"Yes," I replied.

"Good," he said. "Please continue."

And so I read: "They asked him, 'Then who are you? Are you Elijah?' He said, 'I am not' " (1:21).

"Stop again, please. Is this not a second person that the Jews were expecting to appear? The one they call Elijah?"

I anticipated that he might be asking why John the Baptist claimed not to be Elijah when Jesus at a later date clearly stated that he was. But this turned out not to be the object of my questioner's inquiries. He listened politely to my explanation and then asked if we could return to the passage in John 1.

The next phrase took me completely off guard. " 'Are you the Prophet?' He answered, 'No' " (1:21). It was at this point that the Muslim pounced. "Is the word 'Prophet' capitalized in your Bible?" he asked.

Suddenly I knew what was coming. "Then could you please tell me who 'The Prophet' is?" he asked.

I confess that I did not know the answer. I sat for a moment trying to come up with a reply.

"How is it possible that you do not know?" He began to hammer away at me. "Is it because you do not want to admit that your own Book tells about the expectation in the time of Jesus that Prophet Muhammad would come? Explain to me why you

Christians persist in your stubborn refusal to admit that Muhammad was a Prophet sent from God!"

This was only the beginning of a calm and reasoned two-hour session. It included seemingly sincere questions by the Muslims on passages in the Bible that "clearly contradicted" each other. The agenda was brutally clear: Christian beliefs, and particularly those about the Islamic faith, were entirely erroneous. The Muslims repeatedly battered me with aspects of teaching from both the Bible and the Qur'an (the Muslim Scriptures, also commonly spelled "Koran") to which I had no answers. I left that room like a whipped puppy, and the drive home was one of the darkest times of my life. I seriously wondered if I would be able to complete my studies and take up the ministry to Muslims my wife and I had envisioned for our future.

That difficult day, however, turned out to be one of the most important in my life. After time spent in prayer and recovery, I resolved never to be caught on those issues again. Rather than laying down my studies in despair, I increased the pace. I worked harder than ever to answer those questions and others that had not come up during that first session.

To some extent, I have accomplished these objectives. Now I know that Jesus fulfilled the role of the Prophet who was expected by the Jews of the first century. Peter makes this clear in Acts 3:17-22, quoting the passage from which the expectation arose (Deuteronomy 18:15), and at least some people recognized this fact as recorded in John 6:14. I have learned answers to many other objections as well.

I do not, however, consider myself to be an "evangelist to Muslims" in the classic sense of that term. I share with the followers of Islam how I became a Christian and the gospel message about salvation in Jesus alone whenever I get a chance. But I am not, nor do I ever intend to become, a "debater." I am convinced that debates between Christian and Muslim apologists have limited value.

In answering the questions of individual Muslims, I show that I have cared enough about them to spend time learning about their faith and its contrasts to Christianity. While many of my answers have not been satisfactory to the listeners (and perhaps never will be), the mere fact that I *have* answers has often steered a conversation toward significant discussion.

Getting to Know Our Neighbors

One of the chief aims of this book is to share the results of my studies and experiences with Muslims. While I have visited countries such as Egypt and Indonesia where the adherents of Islam form a majority, my relationships with Muslims have been developed mainly in the United States and in Europe. Thus it is my desire to provide a street-level view of the Muslims in America from an evangelical Christian perspective.

Who are these people who are becoming our neighbors, store clerks and service station owners? Are they truly like the terrorists portrayed in the news media who secretly espouse destruction of the World Trade Center or bombing of New York City's subways? The answer is a resounding "no." The Muslims of America are most certainly not terrorists, with rare exceptions. But do the adherents of Islam have an agenda while living in our midst? Some do, and we will look at this agenda.

Carl Ellis and I want to describe the various kinds of Muslims one is likely to encounter in contemporary America. Many are aware of Black Muslims and Middle Eastern Muslims, but few are aware of the varieties among these two large groups of people. In addition, many have yet to encounter White Americans (i.e., Anglo-Saxon Protestants, Catholics and Jews) who have adopted Islam. We will identify and describe as many of the various Muslims that live among us as possible. I will contribute background and general knowledge of Islam in America, and Carl will help readers understand the highly publicized movement of Louis Farrakhan, leader of the organization known as the Nation of Islam.

I should mention at the outset that this book is not intended to introduce all the beliefs and practices of the Islamic faith. The reader will not find here a complete account of the history of Islam or an exposition of each of its main theological propositions. The book does not contain a detailed description of the "Five Pillars" (the *Shahada*, or testimony that "There is no god but Allah, and Muhammad is his Messenger"; the five daily prayers, the fast of Ramadan, the pilgrimage to Mecca and charitable giving).

An increasing number of fine works contain this information from the perspective of Christians and,

of course, from the perspective of Muslims themselves.[1] Readers would find basic knowledge of Islam helpful, but it is not essential to understanding
our main themes. Explanations of specific terms
which might be unfamiliar are provided where necessary.

After describing the Muslims of America from a
variety of standpoints, we will evaluate their religious faith and practices. Muslims claim that theirs
is the one true religion—a claim that all Christians
would vehemently deny. But could it be that Islam—as even some Christians claim—is an alternative path to reaching the One True God? Is it possible that devout Muslims will be accounted
righteous and permitted to enter the kingdom of
heaven? The authors' answer to both of these questions is a definite "no." We believe that the teachings of Islam diverge so much from biblical Christianity that there is no possibility of a Muslim
"stumbling onto" the narrow path that leads to eternal life through reading the Qur'an.

Growing Your Faith—and Your Witness

Finally, Carl and I will provide suggestions on how
to be a Christian witness to Muslims. We believe that
adherents of Islam will be won to Christ not by our
ability to answer their questions and objections, but
through a curiosity and hunger aroused by a biblical
lifestyle. Carl will help us understand the thought processes of African-American Muslims and how to best
deal with their views of life and the world.

I have one further purpose for this volume which may at first seem paradoxical. I want Christians to become more biblical in their faith and more dynamic in their walk with Christ through their studies of Islam. Max Muller, the founding father of the academic discipline known as comparative religious studies, said, "He who knows one knows none." Muller believed that most people have never examined their personal religious faith compared to another world religion. Most have never been challenged to the core of their being regarding their own beliefs.

I agree that learning the beliefs of a Muslim, Hindu, Buddhist or some other religious person is essential for Christians to deepen their understanding of the biblical view of God. Without such a comparative approach, most remain "greenhouse Christians," people who have grown up in a controlled environment and who have difficulty functioning in the world of a multiplicity of religious alternatives. It is our hope that the challenge of Islam will strengthen the commitment of Christians toward their Lord and Savior, Jesus Christ, as well as their appreciation for the plan of salvation set forth in the Bible.

I would like to make it clear that neither Carl nor I write as "experts" regarding ministry to Muslims, if "expert" means a person who has won many Muslims to the Christian faith. I am personally convinced that such "experts" are limited to a handful of persons scattered across the globe. The message of Christianity has almost never been well received among Muslim peoples.

There are, however, an increasing number of Christians who are learning the languages of Muslims, studying their literature, history, doctrine and practices, and getting to know them. As opportunities have arisen, they have witnessed for Christ as much as possible. Carl and I have found such encounters joyous and enriching. It is our hope and prayer that this book will motivate others to immerse themselves in the world of Islam and learn to know that joy as well.

Note

1   My recommendations for such reading are the following: Fazlur Rahman, *Islam*, 2nd Ed. (Chicago: University of Chicago Press, 1979); Frederick Denny, *An Introduction to Islam* (New York: Macmillan Press, 1985); Fazlur Rahman, *Major Themes of the Qur'an* (Minneapolis, MN: Bibliotheca Islamica, 1984); Seyyed Hossein Nasr, *A Young Muslim's Guide to the Modern World* (Chicago: Kazi Publications, 1994); Norman L. Geisler and Abdul Saleeb, *Answering Islam* (Grand Rapids: Baker Book House, 1994); J. Dudley Woodberry, *Muslims and Christians on the Emmaus Road* (Monrovia, CA: MARC Publications, 1989). A more comprehensive listing can be found in the appendix.

Part 1

The Arrival of Muslims
in America

1

The Muslims of America

It is difficult to estimate the precise number of Muslims living in America today. Government census statistics no longer include data on an individual's religious affiliation, and few (if any) organizations have accurately determined the spiritual beliefs of private citizens. Some researchers have produced estimates based on immigration statistics which include the country of one's birth and former residence.

Such an approach could be considered fairly accurate for certain countries. Turkey, for instance, is 99.5 percent Muslim. But men and women who come from Egypt, Jordan, Syria, Lebanon, Israel and Indonesia—to name only a few—might be Christian, Jewish or even (in Indonesia) Buddhist or Hindu.

This approach also does not ascertain the number of *indigenous* Muslims, that is, those people who have converted to Islam while living in America.

This group would include anyone not raised in the Muslim faith who has formally proclaimed the *Shahada* before a group of Muslim officials. This act makes a person an adherent of Islam.

But many mosques and Islamic centers do not keep records of attendance or membership. That seems strange to Christians, who see worship and Sunday school attendance figures posted weekly in church sanctuaries. But many immigrant Muslims come from countries with minimal individual rights and liberties. In such places one learns that the less information available, the better. Organizations that do keep information are reluctant to release it to independent researchers.

For these reasons, current estimates of Muslims living in the United States vary from less than a million to over 9 million. The most commonly accepted figure, however, is 6 million out of a total population of 260 million persons; Muslims thus form only about two percent of the American people. But they are a substantial minority, rivaling in size (though not yet in influence) the Jewish population of the United States. Where have these Muslims come from, and what kinds of lives do they lead in America? We will provide a brief summary here.[1]

How Muslims Arrived

The African slave trade brought the first Muslims to America. In 1717 names such as Omar ibn Said, Job Ben Solomon, Prince Omar and Ben Ali appeared on the manifests of some slave ships arriving on the Atlantic coastline.[2] Owners changed these persons' names after purchase. Since the majority of slaveholders considered themselves "Christian," it is unlikely that they permitted the standard Muslim practices of prayer and fasting. The pilgrimage to Mecca and charitable giving would also have been out of the question.

Within a hundred years of the beginning of slavery in the colonies, Christianity was the only religion consistently practiced by America's slaves. This faith was often forced upon them rather than willingly adopted, which played an important role in the formation and rhetoric of the African-American Nation of Islam more than two centuries later.

Voluntary migrations of Muslims to America began during the late nineteenth century and have been classified into five separate waves.[3] From 1875 to 1912, migration consisted mainly of individuals or families who were escaping difficult political, social or economic situations. Most of the immigrants in this wave came from the rural parts of Syria, Jordan, Palestine and Lebanon. The majority found work in mines and factories. Those of a more independent nature often became peddlers. The majority remained in America and formed small, usually urban Muslim communities.

The second wave from 1918 to 1922 consisted of men and women who sought to escape the depressed conditions of their countries following World War I. A large number, as well as those who came in the third wave from 1930 to 1938, had relatives or acquaintances who had come earlier. The Statue of Liberty in New York City's harbor was meaningful for Christians and Jews who had fled religious persecution and financial hardship in Europe and other lands, but this monument also became—and is still today—a poignant symbol for Muslims. Keep these facts in mind when we later deal with stereotypes of Muslims as terrorists focused on destroying the United States for being "The Great Satan."

The fourth wave followed World War II, yet another period of chaotic living conditions. In addition to the Middle East, individuals arrived from India, Pakistan, Turkey, Eastern Europe, the Soviet Union and other countries. While earlier immigrants had come mainly from rural areas, the fourth wave were mostly urban and often highly educated and well-to-do. Some would have been considered Westernized even before arriving in the United States. Most earlier Muslim immigrants had been more or less forced to assimilate into American culture in order to survive financially and socially. But the new arrivals, having economic resources of their own, were able to retain their traditional values and practices.

The fifth and most recent wave of newcomers began in 1967 as a part of President Lyndon Johnson's Great Society. Quotas had favored Europeans. Now they were relaxed considerably, and immigrants from Africa and Asia began to enter the United States in droves. This trend continues today. Estimates indicate that about 35,000 men and women from the Middle East and North Africa now enter the United States annually.[4] A majority of those entering America today are highly educated professionals.

Where Muslims Live

Where do the Muslims of America live? California (approximately 1 million), New York (800,000), Illinois (420,000), New Jersey (200,000), Indiana (180,000), Michigan (170,000), Virginia (150,000), Texas (140,000), Ohio (130,000) and Maryland (70,000) have the highest immigrant populations.[5] Muslims tend to choose their place of residence for proximity to a major city (Los Angeles, San Diego, New York, Chicago, Washington, D.C.); proximity to factory-oriented jobs (Detroit, Toledo); and climate (the southern states).

While population demographics are becoming increasingly available, compiling a comprehensive profile of Muslims in the United States remains difficult. Since World War II, Muslim immigrants have not "clumped" into cohesive communities as have other groups. Nearly all major cities had or have a Chinatown, Little Italy, Irish quarter or Jewish section. But Muslims have tended to disperse throughout metropolitan areas.

Gatherings at mosques—including the Friday afternoon prayer service, the most important time (theologically) of the Muslim week—are viewed as optional by many Muslims. A visit to one on a Friday afternoon *might* present useful information for a demographer, but it may also be highly skewed. The majority find it impossible to leave work or schools at 1 p.m. on Friday. Families may observe Muslim practices privately, but if their homes are scattered throughout a city, putting together a profile is a daunting task.

The Image of Islam

But there is another more significant reason why a portrait of a "typical Muslim" is hard to come by. The American media has not been kind to the adherents of Islam. It is safe to say that in the 1960s through the 1980s many were reluctant to be openly Muslim for fear of adverse consequences. Television documentaries such as *Death of a Princess* and major motion pictures such as *Not without My Daughter* and *Aladdin* provided ready-made images, and most Muslims have neither the opportunities nor the personal contacts to correct such images.

Nearly everyone in America knows that the Ayatollah Khomeini was a "fanatical" Muslim—and that in 1979 he held several dozen Americans hostage in the U.S. embassy in Iran. Everyone knows that the "Adolf Hitler" of the 1980s and 1990s is Iraq's Saddam Hussein. Everyone knows of the Arab—and hence Muslim—oil embargos of the 1970s. And everyone knows that the World Trade Center was bombed by Middle Eastern terrorists who were Muslims.

Nearly everyone is familiar with the "dark side" of Islam. But only a tiny fraction is aware that, to a very great extent, the scientific and technological superiority of Western civilization comes from the thinking and discoveries of the Muslims during the Medieval Period. Americans owe their standard of living, in large part, to the adherents of Islam. We will look at this "positive side" in more detail at a later time. It suffices for now to note that due to their stereotype, many Muslims are understandably reluctant to mix with other Americans and risk ostracism. They are often quiet and withdrawn, which denies Americans the opportunity to learn that the majority are different from the media image.

African-American Muslims have also suffered from an image problem. Indeed, one could say that they have suffered twice as much as ethnic Muslims. The teachings and practices of Elijah Muhammad, founder of the original Nation of Islam, deviated radically from classic Islam. So the Muslims of the world relegated them to the status of heretics; the label "Muslim" was entirely inappropriate. At the same time, the Nation of Islam was classified for decades as Black sociology and history rather than the more appropriate category of American religious movements. As a result, the majority population of America has not had the opportunity—or has not taken the opportunity—to learn about this highly significant segment of Islam in America.

Recently we have begun to see changes among Americans and Muslims. Increasingly, the more positive side of the Muslim story is being told. Muslims themselves have initiated part of this change. Many have realized that *they* must change the stereotype. Letters appeared in newspapers all over the country protesting Disney's *Aladdin* and the chauvinistic portrayal of Mr. Habib in *Father of the Bride II*. Letters to President Clinton asked that he include Muslims in future comments about America's Judeo-Christian heritage. We read of protests against the media and government officials for jumping to the conclusion that the Oklahoma City bombing was the work of Muslim terrorists and the many apologies that were extended to the Muslim community as a result.

A Closer Look

As Muslims become increasingly visible, we can begin to assemble a generalized profile. We find that Muslims living in North America represent several different social classes and a variety of occupations.

There is Qadri Abdallah, a Palestinian who brought his wife and child to the United States to escape the Arab-Israeli conflict. Qadri worked with me at a sporting goods store in suburban Chicago, where he earned $5 an hour. He attended night school in order to get a higher-paying job and taught Arabic at an Islamic school on weekends. His wife, who always wore distinctive Muslim dress, preferred to stay at home with their young child.

As a single-income family living in greater Chicago, their struggle to survive was not pleasant. They certainly missed their homeland, and the cultural and linguistic barriers must have seemed insurmountable. But Qadri never complained in my hearing; he appeared to be at peace. He was glad to be in America where he could raise his child in comparative safety and security.

Just five miles away from the sporting goods store where Qadri and I worked, the Islamic Center of Greater Chicago stands in the upper-middle class suburb of Northbrook. A lavish mosque complete with dome and minaret, at first glance the structure appears out of place in suburban America, but it has become something of a showpiece. Once a month, the congregation holds a potluck dinner with many Middle Eastern and Eastern European foods. Most who attend are physicians, engineers, middle-level managers and college professors—a different economic level from that of Qadri.

After the meal, participants drift to the Center's elaborate lecture hall, complete with inlaid tiles which trace out verses from the Qur'an. Forums discuss such topics as "Will Islam Thrive in America, or Merely Survive?" Questions posed are the same as those asked in a home Bible study or Sunday school class—with very different answers. Verses of the Qur'an flow freely in Arabic.

Another segment of Islam in America are members of the Muslim Student Association (MSA), a national organization founded in the early 1960s at the Champaign-Urbana campus of the University of Illinois. At Northwestern University, for instance, the number of students involved in this campus group numbers well over 150—at least as large as the Navigators, Campus Crusade or InterVarsity Christian organizations. These young Muslims want to raise their visibility in order to challenge and change the stereotype.

Muhammad Eissa, faculty advisor for the MSA at Northwestern, seeks to help these young people explore the meaning of Islam in the modern world. He desires to see each student established in the Qur'an and classic Islamic theology. He wants to see their "identity crises" resolved.

Finally, there is George, who lives in the Bronx. For several years he was a devoted member of the

Nation of Islam. The impeccable dress—including the bow tie—abstinence from alcohol and tobacco, strictly regulated diet, the work ethic and careful disposition of finances—all characterized George's life. These practices gave meaning to life in the inner city. Although he is no longer a member, he still speaks of the former leader as "the Honorable Elijah Muhammad."

These four examples illustrate the wide variety of individuals scattered across the United States who call themselves Muslims. According to the Islamic Resource Institute of the American Muslim Council, fifty-six percent of the Muslims of America are immigrants, while forty-four percent are native born.

African-Americans comprise nearly 42 percent of the total population. South Asians (including Indian, Pakistani, Bangladeshi, Sri Lankan and Afghan Muslims) make up 24.4 percent, Arabs 12.4 percent, Africans 6.2 percent, Iranians 3.6 percent, Turks 2.4 percent, Southeast Asians 2 percent and Whites 1.6 percent. The remaining 5.6 percent do not fit into a specific ethnic category.[6]

Despite this diversity, some broad categories exist for large numbers of Muslims, enabling us to better understand them. For instance, a definite distinction can be made between what I call *defensive-pacifist* and *offensive-activist* Muslims.

Defensive-Pacifist Muslims

Muslims who are defensive and pacifistic in their essential orientation have come to America with the same motivation that characterized the Irish, Italians and Swedes. All of these sought increased economic opportunities and/or greater political and social freedoms. Muslims who came to America during the first, second and third waves fall mostly into this category. These persons sought the melting pot concept in their lives. They learned the English language as quickly as possible and adopted Western clothing styles. Religious practices which deviated from the Protestant Christian "standard" of America were kept discreet.

This is not to say that these persons absorbed American culture so totally that their Islamicity disappeared. Just as other nationalities formed organizations for the purpose of celebrating and preserving their ethnic distinctions, so did many Muslims. By the early 1960s, a variety of organizations existed in several larger cities.

In New York City alone, one could find the United Nile Valley Association, the Nubian Sudanese Association, the North African American Association, the Pakistan League of America, the Yemen American Society, the Indonesian Association, the Malay American Association, the Moroccan United Organizations Federation and the like. These organizations formed along national lines and also along gender lines, such as the Young Men's Muslim Association and the Muslim Ladies' Cultural Society.[7]

The defensive-pacifist Muslims have been instrumental in establishing mosques and Islamic institutions for the purpose of helping Muslims preserve their Islamicity in the midst of "Christian" America.

Funding for these ventures often comes from Muslim countries such as Egypt, Pakistan and Saudi Arabia, which have large populations in the United States and who feel somewhat responsible for helping to maintain their roots.

But it is one thing to supply funds to build a mosque or Islamic center and quite another to staff such institutions. For the Muslims of America, leadership is a much larger problem than finances. The Islamic centers and mosques have tremendous difficulty employing qualified leaders to give direction and inspiration to those who attend the prayer services and other functions.

It is not difficult to understand how this problem has arisen. In countries where the majority is Muslim, a potent *social pressure* rules. The ostracism that would result from violating a Muslim code, such as a Muslim female attempting to marry a non-Muslim male or converting from Islam to another religious faith, would in many cases make it impossible to live a normal life.

In some lands, the official punishment for apostasy is death. For theft, amputation of the right hand. For unfaithfulness in marriage—on the part of the wife, at least—divorce or even death. In any of these cases, a sundering of family relationships, loss of employment or loss of inheritance might result. Such stringent measures form invisible fences which make an authoritarian leadership structure almost superfluous. The majority do what they are supposed to do because the alternative is too harsh to endure.

But this kind of social pressure does not exist in America. Those who come from lands with social and political pressures notice the difference if not immediately, then eventually. This has become problematic for many Muslim groups. They lack a uniform society and, in many cases, an authoritative voice to help control their actions, speech and choices. While many are aware that they need to avoid the dangers of over-assimilation, they do not know what is too much. To what extent should they hold on to the customs and practices of their homeland? At what point does assimilation jeopardize Islamicity? These are highly subjective questions, and Muslims find little to help them with the answers.

Defensive-pacifist Muslims have a minimal desire to convert Americans to Islam. It is in this sense that they are "pacifistic." They are content to pursue their occupations, raise their families and take part in the same leisure activities as other Americans. They desire to be accepted by mainstream society and hesitate to do anything which might point to them as outsiders. They vehemently oppose media stereotypes which portray Muslims as terrorists or as backward camel-riders. They simply ask that America's civil liberties—including the freedom of religion—extend to them as well. These latter characteristics have led us to characterize them as "defensive."

Offensive-Activist Muslims

The majority of those who come from a traditionally Islamic country such as Saudi Arabia, Egypt,

Turkey or Pakistan may fall within the defensive-pacifist category. Many locations, however, are seeing a slow but significant shift toward the activist orientation. *Offensive*-activist Muslims do not aim to *offend* people. Rather, these Muslims seek to propagate their faith and persuade Americans to abandon their current religious beliefs or secular lifestyle and convert to Islam. These Muslims are convinced that their main purpose is to function as missionaries to "the lost": secular, Christian and Jewish Americans. They believe that Islam is the only valid path to salvation and that non-Muslims will be condemned on the Judgment Day to an eternal existence in the Fire.

While Muslims are often seen as having political goals of territorial conquest, this is not the case with most activists in America. A majority believe that Christianity and Judaism once contained the fullness of God's revelation, but since the advent of Muhammad and the Qur'an, Islam has superseded these faiths. For those who are convinced of the historical decline of Christianity and Judaism, activism is religiously—not politically— motivated.

Activist Muslims have refused to assimilate into American society. They tend to condemn defensive-pacifist Muslims for having succumbed to materialism and secularism. Within this group would be the student populations of large universities who reside in the United States only temporarily. Societal acceptance is a low priority. Such a mentality gives these Muslims greater freedom to criticize America and to function in missionary fashion.

In addition to the students, many immigrants entering the United States currently were committed to activism in their country of origin. They simply continue their activities—as much as possible—in their adopted homeland. Other immigrants would have been considered "nominal" Muslims in their home country. But upon their arrival, an interesting psychological change occurs. Sometimes an encounter with an American who—intentionally or unintentionally—insults or degrades the Islamic faith may cause a Muslim to "dig his heels in," as it were. Motivated by an "I'll show him" attitude, such a person often becomes more pronouncedly Muslim than he ever was in the homeland.

He consults Muslim leaders, studies the Qur'an and Muslim theology, attends mosque—and Islam obtains a vice-grip. For other Muslims, no specific encounter gives rise to their renewed zeal. It comes from a gradual awareness of the vast ethical differences between American and Muslim cultures. Haddad and Lummis have done an excellent job of charting this growth in awareness in their book *Islamic Values in the United States,* noting that Muslims in general consider their own system of values to be vastly superior to that of "Christian America."[8]

As the motivation for much Islamic activism is a sincere desire to turn people away from eternal punishment, it is difficult to disagree that American society is highly immoral. Evangelical Christians in particular have been saying that for decades. But it is ironic that individuals who in many cases are only nominally Muslim when they arrive are often made more radically Muslim by their contact with American society.

Activist Muslims are beginning to flex their collective muscle. The growth of mosques has outpaced the growth in population. In 1960, 104 Muslim places of worship existed in the United States; in 1993, they had surpassed 1,100. And as the Muslim population grows, the influence of the Islamic community grows. In Los Angeles, the Islamic center has petitioned the public school system to revise textbooks which distort the history of Islam and portray Muslims as "backward, warlike camel-riders."

Muslims in Chicago are seeking to have Friday, the holy day for Muslims, declared an official "weekend" day for members of the Islamic faith. They point out that most Americans are not required to work on Saturday and Sunday, the holy days of Jews and Christians respectively. As the population of Muslims in America approaches that of the Jewish people (some claim it has already surpassed them), they argue that Muslims should be allowed to celebrate their holy day as well. The same applies to Muslim holidays, such as the *Eid al-Fitr* and the *Eid al-Adha*. Again, since Jewish holidays are officially celebrated with school and business closings in many sections of the United States, the "Eids" should also be made official holidays.

In addition, some Muslims argue that America's constitutional guarantee of religious freedom should allow for special concessions for fasting and prayer for Muslim students and employees during the month of Ramadan. Some Muslims are even petitioning local public school boards to conform toilet facilities to the requirements of Muslim law. It is often argued that if buildings are modified to allow access and mobility to handicapped persons, then, out of respect for their religious beliefs, concessions should be made for Muslims.

The activists of America know that Muslims participating in many small and scattered organizations will not cause American society to make significant changes. Thus they have banded together to form larger organizations to put forth their agendas. Perhaps the largest is the Islamic Society of North America, founded in 1983 as an outgrowth of the Muslim Student Association (MSA). Since 1962, MSA had grown rapidly to include other individuals besides students. In 1982 a branch organization called the Muslim Communities Association formed to meet the needs of former students who had remained in America.

Other agencies, such as the Association of Muslim Social Scientists, the Association of Muslim Scientists and Engineers and the Islamic Medical Association came about to present a united voice to speak for common interests. Annual conventions provide a forum for social and cultural issues, scientific and technological endeavors, and medical ethics, to name only a few topics.

Some Common Ground

Because of the diversity in such a spectrum of organizations, the Islamic Society of North America (ISNA) became an umbrella agency to oversee and give direction. ISNA oversees the Islamic Book Service (also known as the North American Islamic Trust), the Islamic Teaching Center and the Foundation for International Development. The Teaching Center is responsible for *da'wah* (missionary) activities among young people and arranges everything from summer camps to neighborhood Qur'an studies. This agency also serves to the incarcerated in a style similar to Charles Colson's Prison Fellowship Ministries.

The Foundation for International Development sends aid to famine or disaster-stricken countries, much like the evangelical agency World Relief and Compassion International. ISNA is a comprehensive organization, duplicating in large measure the work of some of the more well-known Christian parachurch ministries. Like these agencies, ISNA is at least national, if not global, in its purpose and scope.

Muslims are still developing their collective functioning in North America, but make no mistake: they are making rapid strides. In the latest edition of *Islamic Horizons*—the Muslim equivalent of *Christianity Today*—I found advertisements for a number of organizations which reflect nearly every conceivable area of today's society. These groups include the following:

> *The Amana Mutual Funds Trust*—a brokerage firm offering growth and income funds. The advertisement lists the North American Islamic Trust as the agency's "religious consultant."

Ebrahim Lunat, Certified Public Accountant—a CPA who offers to help with tax planning and preparation from a Muslim point of view.

The Islamic Da'wah at Universities—a new Muslim campus organization that also arranges pilgrimages to Mecca in Saudi Arabia.

The Crescent Publishing House—a Muslim publisher currently soliciting questions from young Muslim girls about "belief, *salah* [prayer], fasting, *zakah* [charitable giving], hajj [the pilgrimage], *jihad,* the Qur'an, *hadith* [Muslim traditions], *fiqh* [law], the rights of parents, husband, wife, children, marriage, dating, or *hijab* [head covering], etc." The agency is collecting these questions to include in *A Handbook for Young Muslim Girls.*

The Islamic Medical Association of North America—announcing its 1997 convention in Amman, Jordan.

The Caravan Xpress—advertising itself as "Your Islamic Home Shopping Service," it offers "high quality Islamic fashions for the entire family," including jewelry, cosmetics and home decorations.

The Indian Muslim Relief Committee—a subdivision of the Islamic Society of North America which has as its goal the feeding and education of 24,500 poverty-stricken families in India.

The Islamic Book Service—which offers books, cassette tapes, videos and computer software on Islam-related topics.

Midamar Corporation—which sells "highest quality *halal* meats," which means meats prepared according to Islamic law.

UFI, Inc.—an agency based in Boulder, Colorado, which advertises "da'wah checks." These are bank checks with pictures of Islamic mosques, a shrine in Mecca and other places of importance in the world of Islam. The advertisement exhorts one to "Make Da'wah with every check you write!" In other words, be a witness for Islam by writing checks which contain pictures of Islamic shrines.

Ideal Travel—a travel agency which arranges the pilgrimage to Mecca.

The above list is just a small indication of how Muslims are building a subculture of growing influence. As Christians, we cannot afford to ignore these dedicated men and women who are perhaps our chief competitors in the cosmic struggle for the souls of lost human beings.

Notes

1 For detailed information concerning the origins of Muslims in America, see Yvonne Yazbeck Haddad, ed., *The Muslims of America* (New York: Oxford University Press, 1991); Yvonne Yazbeck Haddad and Adair T. Lummis, *Islamic Values in the United States: A Comparative Study* (New York: Oxford University Press, 1987) and Yvonne Yazbeck Haddad and Jane Idleman Smith, *Muslim Communities in North America* (Albany, NY: State University of New York Press, 1994). As one might discern from this list,

Yvonne Haddad of Georgetown University is the leading re-
searcher with regard to Islam in America.

2   See Beverlee Turner Mehdi, *The Arabs in America 1492-1977*
(New York: Oceana Publications, 1978), 1-2. See also Allen D.
Austin, ed., *African Muslims in Ante-Bellum America: A Sourcebook*
(New York: Garland Publishing, 1984).

3   See Haddad and Lummis, *Islamic Values*, 13-14.

4   Estimates regarding immigration are difficult due to the fact that
immigrants to the U.S. are no longer classified by religious affiliation. But in 1991, for instance, there were over 100,000 legal immigrants from Pakistan, India, Egypt, Bangladesh, Iran and
Lebanon. Since the populations of each of these countries is over-
whelmingly Muslim, it is almost a certainty that a substantial percentage of those who arrived in the United States from these
countries were Muslim. Therefore the figure of 35,000 per year
may well be quite conservative. See Richard Bernstein, "A
Growing Islamic Presence: Balancing Sacred and Secular," *New
York Times*, Sunday, 2 May 1993, A26.

5   Nick Galifianakis, "U.S. Muslim Population Grows," *Rockland
Journal-News* (Nyack, New York), 10 February 1994, C4.

6   Ibid.

7   Mahmoud Youssef Shawarbi's *Al-Islam w'al-Muslimun fi'l-Qara
al-Amrikiyya* (Cairo: Dar al-Qalam, 1963), 7, contains an extensive listing of these organizations.

8   Haddad and Lummis, *Islamic Values*.

2

The "Gospel"
According to Islam

As we noted in the previous chapter, it is mainly the activist Muslims who seek to win Americans to the religion of Islam. Their desire to be "missionaries" (or *da'is*, as they are called in Arabic, a word derived from a verb meaning "to call" or "to invite") has come from at least two separate sources. Some history is required in order to understand these motivations.

An ongoing debate among scholars questions whether Muhammad intended Islam to become a worldwide religion. Many claim that political aspirations motivated him, and he created a faith designed to unite the scattered tribes of the Arabian peninsula. A majority, however, scoff at this idea. They say that nothing in Muhammad's earlier years even remotely resembles political designs. But whatever the founder's intentions, Muhammad's successors' intent was to spread the faith over the entire known world. Thus, Islam became a supremely missionary religion.

Once the Muslims began their expansion outside of Arabia after Muhammad's death, the religion spread quickly across the Middle East, North Africa, Spain, parts of Eastern Europe and eastward to India. The original westward expansion halted in A.D. 732 at the battle of Tours in France, and the eastward expansion ceased at about the same time on the Indian subcontinent. For the most part, that was the end of it. With the exception of Indonesia, Malaysia and some parts of the Philippines and eastern Africa, very little territory has been added to the Islamic world since 732.

But within 100 years, the adherents of Islam had conquered a greater geographical area in a shorter amount of time than any other group in history. When asked how their forefathers were able to achieve such success, contemporary Muslims will not attribute it to military skill or religious devotion. They will simply claim that the will and aid of Allah made their victories possible.

Age of Advancement

The centuries following the *jihads* have been considered a period of maintenance and consolidation. During this time, the chief goals were the establishment of Muslim institutions and the education of conquered peoples in the doctrines and practices of Islam. This period, spanning the centuries from A.D. 800-1200, is generally known as the "classical" age of Muslim history. Tremendous advances were made in the areas of science, mathematics, literature, art, architecture, navigation, astronomy and the like during this time.

Most Americans are unaware that when the Muslims conquered the Middle East and North Africa, they acquired a large number of resources left over from ancient Greek and Roman civilizations. The thinking of several Western philosophers, including Socrates, Plato and Aristotle, was studied and incorporated into the Islamic worldview.

Principles of rationalism and linear thinking combined with indigenous Arab ideas to form the foundation of what we today call "the liberal arts and sciences." The decimal point—a product of Muslim civilization—opened the door to modern mathematics. The algebraic system of mathematics comes from *al-jabr*, an Arabic term which contains the idea of "a predestined, inescapable decree of fate." This implies the surety of mathematics. Chemistry, including the original lists of the table of elements, finds its roots in Islam. The Arabs called this *al-kemi*, from which the West derived "alchemy" and finally "chemistry." Partly because of their geographic expansion, the Muslims became expert mapmakers and in the course of their journeying invented several instruments of navigation.

Many consider the literature from this time period to be exquisite, with contributions such as *The Tales of a Thousand and One Nights*. In the field of architecture, Muslims perfected the use of the dome for their mosque structures, developing techniques for wedding a round structure to a square tower. All in all, there were few fields of knowledge left untouched during this 400-year period, and Muslims are credited with founding the world's first university in the tenth century. Located in Cairo, Egypt, and known as *al-Azhar*, this school still exists today.

At this point, many readers may be scratching their heads in puzzlement. They may be asking: if all these developments were Muslim in origin, why do the Muslims today not lead in science and technology? When—and how—did Western civilization surpass the world of Islam in all of the areas? The answer is an interesting one.

Time of Devotion

In the early 1200s—in the midst of Islam's maintenance and consolidation period—the Muslim world was invaded by the Mongols, barbarian raiders who swept out of eastern Asia and conquered many countries quickly. The Mongols were not stopped until they reached the borders of Turkey and Palestine. In the course of these conquests, hundreds of thousands of the adherents of Islam were killed, enslaved or displaced. Many of the religion's greatest minds found such devastation highly problematic. Chief among the questions being raised was this: if indeed the Muslims were the people most favored by God—as evidenced by the original *jihadic* victories over so much of the known world—then why had God allowed the Mongol infidels to achieve such success?

This question had a limited number of answers. One possibility, of course, was that God had never really been on the side of the Muslims; their original conquests were due to luck and their own military skills. But this was not a comfortable thought, for it left open the possibility that nothing more than chance rules the lives of humans. If so, no God reigns over the universe. There is no afterlife and no hope. Muslims rejected this possibility as untenable.

There was left, then, conjecture that God was using the Mongols to discipline or punish the Muslim world for some grievous act of sin. In the Qur'an one finds accounts of such events; perhaps this was only the latest in a long line of harsh—but necessary—dealings with frail and corruptible human beings. But assuming that this was the correct explanation for the Mongol invasions, for what sins were Muslims being punished?

After much thought and debate, they decided their fascination with the arts and sciences during the classical period was the only logical answer. God was displeased that humans had the temerity to think that they could understand His world—or that they would waste time on such studies; time should be devoted to more spiritual endeavors. Many concluded that studies of the Qur'an and Islamic theology were the only worthwhile pursuits for those who wished to please God.

Consequently most (though not all) Muslims began to draw back from classical learning and to simplify their focus in life. Reading the Qur'an (or hearing it read), participating in the five daily prayers and the monthlong fast of Ramadan, becoming prosperous in one's occupation and tending to one's family affairs became the limits of the Muslim lifestyle. In much of the Islamic world, this is still the case today.

Muslim Roots of the Renaissance

Just prior to the Mongol invasions, the exploits known as the Crusades took place. They began with the mission launched by Pope Urban II in A.D. 1096. Although they never accomplished the overall objective of wresting the Holy Land from the hands of the "Mohammedans," some of the Crusaders managed to return to Europe with spoils of war. These included, in many cases, books taken from the personal or institutional libraries of the Muslims of Palestine and Syria. The wealth of knowledge gained by Muslims was translated into European languages. This knowledge became the focus of studies which led to the establishment of the university system of higher learning in Europe.

The Muslim ideas sparked what we today call the Renaissance—the rebirth of Europe out of the superstitious worldview of the Dark Ages. The Renaissance led to tremendous advances by Western Europeans in particular. It allowed them to lay the foundations of "the modern world"—by which is usually meant a technology-oriented civilization based upon philosophical rationalism and scientific methodology. Thus, in a sense, the peoples of the West are forever indebted to the Muslims for the heightened standard of living that we all enjoy.

There was a by-product of these events, however. While Muslims sought to recover from the Mongol invasions and rebuild their civilization into a theologically oriented society, the original goal of worldwide expansion was all but forgotten. Dealing with internal divisiveness over theology and with continued outside invasions absorbed the time and resources of Muslim leaders in their successive regimes.

After the sixteenth century, when Western (European) civilization launched its own expansionist endeavors, the Islamic world began to lose ground. During the seventeenth, eighteenth and nineteenth centuries, Great Britain, France, Germany, Holland and other nations made inroads into Muslim territory. They exercised varying amounts of sovereignty over many of the Muslim peoples of the world.

Early Activism

Near the end of the nineteenth century, Muslim voices in the Middle East began to sound. They called for Islamic nations to do whatever necessary to regain the independence and strength that they had enjoyed before falling under Western sovereignty. They challenged the Muslims of the world to throw off the chains of imperialism and band together under a philosophy which became known as *pan-Islamism.* The fiery speeches, pamphlets and books produced by some of the more radical Muslims inspired several young men in particular. Some of these spoke not only of throwing off the shackles of the West from nations that were already Muslim, but also of how Muslims could resume the original goal of building a worldwide kingdom of Islam.

Some present-day activists have gotten caught up in these ideas and have produced several localized movements which collectively might be called an Islamic "revival." The initiators of these renewal movements are often called "Islamic fundamentalists" because one of their goals is to persuade Muslims everywhere to return to the foundational teachings of Islam. Since one of the original goals of the first Muslims was to spread Islam as far and as fast as possible, modern activists have adopted this as one of their causes as well.

College students—such as those involved in the various chapters of the Muslim Student Association—are particularly interested in returning to this original emphasis on *da'wah*. The idea of winning the world to Islam gives them a *mission*. It is the first time that they have had a *cause*; a reason to live, and the task at hand fills their time. They attend meetings, they dream, they discuss, they plan.

They speak about their religious beliefs to roommates, classmates and friends in the dormitory. They pray in public, and some of the women wear head scarves. They arrange seminars to inform non-Muslims about Islam and to educate nominal Muslims in the activist aspects of their heritage. In short, many of the students from Muslim lands (who usually lived undirected lives there) become "radicalized" through their contact with the activist Muslims of America.

But there is another motivation for activism that affects the young and the more mature as well. The increasing number of Qur'an studies and forums have helped Muslims become aware that they are not living in the U.S. for legitimate reasons. From the standpoint of the Qur'an, economic and political advantages are not justification for moving to the West to live in a country which is not a part of the *dar al-Islam* (the House of Islam). According to Islamic law, a Muslim is not allowed to live in a non-Muslim country for any extended period of time. The only exceptions to this ruling are for persons conducting business, diplomats, missionaries, students and tourists. In all these cases, the stay is expected to be temporary, and the Muslim is to return to the *dar al-Islam*.[1]

"Illegal" Immigration?

The Muslims who immigrated to America during the five waves did not, with few exceptions, come for any of these purposes. Few came with the intention of being only temporary residents, and most were unaware that Islamic law forbids such migrations. Even if they did know, the economic or political perils in their homelands were so great that the drive to survive overruled. But when jobs and homes were secure and they began to feel relatively comfortable in their adopted land, there was time to reflect upon the implications of their change from a religious point of view.

While some have been troubled because they have transgressed the *Shari'a* (the code by which all Muslims are to live), it is doubtful that many Muslims have actually felt any degree of guilt. It is even more doubtful that many would choose to emigrate back to their homelands. The living conditions in most of these countries are so much poorer that a return is practically unthinkable. This is particularly true of second- and third-generation Muslims who have grown up accustomed to the luxuries of the American lifestyle.

There are others, however, who think and ask about the legitimacy of living in a non-Muslim nation. Some have justified remaining by proposing that, in certain ways, the free enterprise systems of American and European democracies are actually closer to Islamic ideals than lands traditionally considered to be Muslim. When this is the case, it is argued, such countries become legitimate places of residence for Muslims.[2]

This reasoning is unsatisfactory for many, however. Some Muslim teachers are giving immigrants another means for continuing residence. According to Islamic law, Muslims may reside in non-Muslim lands if they function as *missionaries* seeking to propagate and establish the teachings of Islam. As long as individuals can say they are involved in some kind of *da'wah* ("missionary") activity, it is acceptable for them to remain in whatever land they have chosen to be home.

So whether it is part of a worldwide Islamic "revival" or justification for continuing residence in a non-Muslim country, an increasing number of American Muslims believe that it is their responsibility to resume the original Islamic goal of worldwide expansion. For Muslims living in the United States, the obvious places to begin are in their neighborhoods and communities. In what ways are they communicating "the gospel according to Islam"?

Muslim Missionary Strategy

Generally speaking, Muslims in contemporary American society implement virtually the same missionary strategies that evangelical Christians use to witness to others about their faith. The use of such strategies has necessitated significant changes on the part of the adherents of Islam, for originally the faith was spread through the *jihad*—a missionary philosophy very different from that of modern Christians.

The concept of *jihad* is usually misunderstood. Almost always translated "holy war," it conveys an image of an Arab horseman with raised sword galloping across the deserts of the Middle East and North Africa. He demands that all non-Muslims convert to Islam or suffer the consequence, usually said to be death. Some Christian apologists characterize the spread of Christianity as a movement of love, whereas Islam's expansion was an act of war. But such a description differs vastly from history.

In the first place, Christianity's advance throughout the world was not bloodless. During the Middle Ages, the conquests of central and northern Europe under Charlemagne, the first "Holy Roman Emperor," and his successors were far more like what we think of as the *jihads* than were the actual *jihads,* in most cases. Further examples of Christian "holy wars" include the Crusades, the wars between

Catholics and Protestants (and in some cases, between Protestants and Protestants) which followed the Reformation in the sixteenth and seventeenth centuries, and the conquest of South America by the European conquistadores. Today's Christians consider such events to be a blight on Christianity, but educated Muslim apologists are quick to mention them.

Controversy exists regarding the motivation behind the Muslims' original missionary strategy. Some scholars believe that the *jihads* were nothing more than territorial conquests for power and wealth, with a religious justification tacked on. Others hold that the early Muslims sincerely desired to bring peace on earth by introducing all peoples to Islam. The word "islam" comes from the Arabic verb *salama,* which means "to submit to" or "to make peace with"; thus a Muslim is one who has submitted to and made peace with God.

The term *"jihad"* actually comes from the Arabic *jahada*, which means "to strive" or "to exert oneself." War is, of course, an extreme means of exerting oneself; but in theory *jihad* does not necessarily involve bloodshed. In the course of expansion, emissaries from Muslim lands went to non-Muslim rulers to issue a *da'wah*, an invitation to submit to the new religion and join the kingdom of Islam. All who submitted were promised material well-being, including the protection of the Muslim military and significantly lower taxes than those of the Christian Byzantines.[3] They also received the opportunity to attain eternal life in *al-Janna*, the garden paradise described in the Qur'an which is the destiny of all Muslims in good standing with God.

The emissaries also made it clear that Muslim law permits Christians and Jews to retain their religious beliefs and practices while submitting to Muslim authority. Monotheists were not required to convert to Islam. Instead, a special social status designated them as *ahl al-dhimma*, or "protected peoples." Persons in this category were required to pay a special tax (the *jizya*) and did not enjoy all the liberties and privileges of Muslim citizens. Still, many Christians and Jews deemed *dhimmi* status to be a happy alternative to conversion to Islam and continued subjection to the Byzantine Empire. The *da'wah* itself often initiated a change of allegiance from a non-Muslim to a Muslim government.

Not all of the groups that the Muslims encountered were so compliant, of course. Bloodshed did occur, though never on the scale alleged by some history books and by most stereotypes. The Berber peoples of North Africa, for instance, proved to be highly resistant to Muslim conquest, and the sword was much in evidence at that time.

Whether a people submitted to the Muslim warriors willingly or unwillingly, basically the same procedure followed. When the Muslim *mujahidun* (people who participate in *jihad*) initially settled in a new territory, they first built small, fortlike enclaves known as garrison cities. Visitors to Cairo, for instance, usually tour al-Fustat, the section which was the original garrison city of Egypt. These cities served two purposes. They kept Muslim soldiers together to squelch any revolts from the subjected peoples. But perhaps even more important was the desire to keep the soldiers—who were mostly new or uneducated Muslims—from mingling with the conquered population and having their faith diluted by the pagan masses.

Once these garrison cities were established, the Muslims began to form the infrastructure of an Islamic nation. They established political, economic, judicial, moral, educational and religious systems. Christians and Jews who had not converted to Islam could retain their separate lifestyles and institutions, but they were not allowed to add to existing churches or synagogues.

The Christians and Jews who made up a majority of the populations of North Africa and the Middle East were allowed to go about their everyday lives with varying levels of normalcy.[4] But if this was indeed the case, how did Muslims expect to expand the kingdom of Islam any more than geographically? The answer reveals a great deal of ingenuity on the part of the original missionary strategists.

Conversion by Absorption

While Jews and Christians in conquered lands were technically allowed to continue with their lifestyles and worldviews, their children and grandchildren grew up in an environment largely formed by Muslim institutions. The government and the chief officials were Muslim; and the culture's economic, judicial, moral and educational systems were all controlled by Muslims. While *dhimmis* were allowed their own systems of justice and education, young people soon learned that persons who converted to Islam fared better educationally, financially, socially and politically than those who did not.

As the first generation of Christians and Jews passed away, their sons and daughters' commitment to the religion of their upbringing waned. Young people *absorbed* Islam from their surroundings, and the beliefs of their parents and grandparents increasingly seemed out-of-date and irrelevant. After just two or three generations, forced conversion was not an issue. The descendants of Jews and Christians voluntarily changed their allegiance from the religion of their heritage to the religion of their current world.

In this way, Islam became solidly entrenched in the countries to which it was brought in the seventh and eighth centuries. Maybe the Muslims had learned lessons from the historical accounts of early Christians who observed that the "blood of the martyrs is the seed of the Church." Perhaps they realized that to come down hard on either Christianity or Judaism would only make the adherents more firmly committed to their heritages.

Or perhaps they were simply forced to adopt this strategy because they were, at the beginning, no more than tiny minorities within most of the lands they conquered. They lacked the strength necessary to bring about and maintain mass conversions. Whatever the reason, they hit upon the perfect strategy for producing converts in a way which made apostasy from the newly chosen faith almost an impossibility.

It should be immediately clear that as historically effective as this strategy once was, it is no longer feasible for Muslims today. Modern Islamic nations lack both the manpower and the technology necessary to conquer non-Muslim nations. Many no longer see territorial expansion as a viable option. Instead, they believe that Muslims should remain in the consolidation and maintenance mode of the past, concentrating upon keeping Islam alive and growing in the territory that its adherents currently control.

But others disagree. They claim that even if the original strategy is no longer possible, Muslims are still responsible to win the world to Islam. Therefore new strategies are needed. And where could such strategies be found? Within Christianity, another of the great missionary religions of the world.

Finding New Strategies

During the nineteenth century, a great deal of Christian missionary activity was directed toward the Muslim world. Several Protestant denominations in Europe and America sent missionaries to the Middle East, North Africa and Asia. Others commissioned by nondenominational "faith" missionary agencies soon followed. By the early twentieth century, it was primarily the members of this latter group—men and women sent out by what became known as parachurch organizations—who accomplished what Muslims desired for themselves: the conversion of individuals to what was believed to be the one true faith. Some began to duplicate the organizations and strategies of Christians.

Establishing this new form of missionary activity has been slow, but it has gained a great deal of momentum during the last three decades. The reasons for the slow start were two. First, many tradition-minded Muslims were suspicious of introducing any new concepts of outreach into Islam since the Qur'an seemed to sanction only the *jihad* as a missionary method.

The Muslim view of the inspiration of the Qur'an and its importance for decision-making within life situations is in many ways much more strict than the view of most Christians. So for these persons the spread of Islam must be by the *jihad* only. The problem with such a traditionalist approach is, of course, that until the *jihad* becomes a possibility, the religion will remain stagnant. And as long as it is stagnant, the possibility of ever regaining the military might necessary for the *jihad* is virtually nil.

Gradually, however, the hesitation to adopt Christian methods of outreach is being overcome. This occurs usually by an appeal to the *hadith*, the traditions of Islam regarding the sayings and practices of Muhammad. Certain pronouncements of the prophet are being reinterpreted to justify new ways of taking the religion to the peoples of the world. Muhammad made a distinction, for instance, between what he called the "Greater *Jihad*" and the "Lesser *Jihad*." The latter concept refers to physical, territorial conquest. The Greater *Jihad*—obviously the more important of the two—involves the struggle of each individual person to master himself.

Using this distinction, it becomes a fairly simple matter to show that the founder of Islam saw the territorial *jihad* as a concept *inferior* to that of an individual changing internally. Thus one can maintain that a missionary strategy which emphasizes individual conversion and inner transformation is justifiable from the standpoint of Islamic tradition. Indeed, such a strategy may justifiably be viewed as *superior* to that of the original *jihads.*

Sufism

Another reason for the slowness of an Islamic outreach strategy is that Muslims had no missionary institutions. Westerners usually consider the Muslim mosque to be equivalent to a Christian church or a Jewish synagogue, both of which hold educational and social functions as well as purely religious activities. But the mosque has traditionally served as a place for worship—in particular, the reading of the Qur'an and the daily prayers. Orthodox Islam has not contained institutions designed for what Christians call "outreach." Only one branch of the faith, Sufism, has ever organized itself for such a purpose.

Sufism has grown up alongside and in some ways complements orthodox Islamic institutions. In other ways, however, the movement diametrically opposes them. Almost from the beginning, a minority of mystically inclined Muslims have been convinced that traditional Islam places entirely too much emphasis upon doctrine, liturgy and ritual, all of which are seen as externally oriented items. For these Muslims, true Islam has more to do with one's inner self; it has to do with matters of the heart and mind rather than with prostrations and pilgrimages. Individuals convinced of this approach gathered disciples into small groups for purposes of teaching and fellowship, and these groups assumed a missionary role as well. They were particularly effective in northern and eastern Africa and in the Indian subcontinent.

Many Sufi groups can be appropriately compared to Roman Catholic orders such as the Franciscans, Dominicans and Jesuits, all of which operate within the confines of the Catholic organizational structure but which enjoy a measure of autonomy as well. Since its inception, Sufism has been relatively successful in spreading the Muslim faith by completely different means than the *jihad*. This movement emphasizes the preaching of the "gospel of Islam," the education of Muslims regarding the knowledge of God and quiet contemplation of spiritual realities. Because of its strong tradition of outreach, modern innovators of a new Islamic missiology have borrowed freely from Sufi practices.

Two men led the way in laying aside the historical emphasis upon the *jihads* in favor of a more individually oriented approach. These men were Hasan al-Banna (1906-1949), the Egyptian founder of the Muslim Brotherhood (the *Ikhwan al-Muslimun*); and Abul A'la Mawdudi (1903-1979), the Indian-born founder of The Islamic Society (the *Jama'at i-Islami*). Both of these men received heavy doses of Sufi influence in their youth, and both desired to see a revival of the original expansionary ideals of Islam. Through their writings, speeches and political activities, these two set the stage for the modern missionary movement of the Muslim world.

"Paramosque" Organizations

As we noted earlier, the institution of the mosque was not equipped to launch missionary endeavors, and so it became necessary to develop new organizations. Like Christian parachurch agencies, paramosque institutions consist of individuals interested either in accomplishing a specific goal or activity or in preserving national, ethnic or theological distinctives. The list of agencies included in chapter 1 (i.e., the Young Men's Muslim Association and the Nile Valley Association) contains several examples of both of these types of institutions.

In the United States, hundreds of paramosque organizations have developed. One can use the same distinction discussed in the first chapter between defensive-pacifists and offensive-activists to categorize paramosque agencies. Some are defensive in orientation, seeking to preserve and defend the cultural trappings of various groups of Muslims, while others take the offensive, planning strategies to win North Americans to Islam.

Challenged by the rapid multiplication of paramosque agencies, many mosques in America have undergone transformations as well. In order to meet the variety of needs of American Muslim communities, some have moved away from being strictly houses of prayer and have taken on other functions. Thus one finds today that mosques are also educational centers, political forums, social halls, informal law courts and counseling clinics. To distinguish themselves from simple mosques, many of these multiplex agencies are called Islamic centers. While all Islamic centers function at certain times as mosques, not all mosques engage in the same breadth of activities.

The leaders or superintendents of mosques, traditionally called *imams*, have undergone a role transformation as well. In the Muslim heartland, the *imam* has historically functioned as a prayer leader and on occasion as a preacher, but usually nothing more than this. As the director of an Islamic center, however, an *imam* is also an educator, administrator, accountant, fund-raiser, political agitator, informal lawyer and counselor.

Obviously it is difficult for any one individual to fulfill such varying roles. Burnout, the mental and physical exhaustion which has unfortunately become fairly common among Christian pastors in America, is no less common within the institutions of Islam. Indeed, the stress is compounded because many *imams* come from other countries. They are attempting to adjust to a new culture and language while performing their duties.

Muslim Da'wah Techniques

Muslims have adopted most—if not all—of the techniques Christians have developed to reach "unbelievers." During the last century, Muslims have themselves been the targets of Christian evangelism. Although they do not have a tradition of personal evangelism, they have learned a great deal from watching their opponents in action.

Indirect da'wah

The current outreach techniques of Muslims can be divided into two main groupings. The first might be termed *indirect da'wah*: the equivalent of what Christians call "lifestyle evangelism." Proponents of this approach use as their chief justification the quranic prohibition against "forcing" others to adopt a religious faith, found in Sura 2:256. This style of outreach has the benefit of allowing the Muslim witness to keep a lower profile than would a ministry of open-air preaching or door-to-door evangelism.

Inviting non-Muslims to observe one's lifestyle will have the effect of breaking down such barriers—assuming, of course, that one's lifestyle is sufficiently exemplary. Such an approach requires that Muslims keep their individual lives in much stricter conformity to the precepts of Islam than they might otherwise feel responsible to do. All people tend to behave more carefully when they know that others are watching.

Another concept which would come under the heading of indirect *da'wah* is that of "Islamization," a term used to describe a method of educating Muslims and non-Muslims alike regarding the principles of the Islamic faith. For instance, the International Institute of Islamic Thought (IIIT), an organization headquartered in a Washington, D.C. suburb in Herndon, Virginia, writes, publishes and markets textbooks which give an Islamic viewpoint on every major academic discipline. The goal is to produce high-quality books for use in major universities and colleges all over America.

The primary focus of such works would be to show how well the Islamic faith accords with the discoveries and needs of the modern world, but they would also contain enough information to enable any interested student to become a Muslim. Robert Crane, an American convert to Islam who works closely with the IIIT, anticipates the creation of a computerized databank as a supplement to the textbooks. This databank would contain an Islamic answer or solution to every conceivable question regarding politics, economics, law, morality and so on.[5]

While the IIIT works mainly in higher education, other Muslim organizations work with youths of elementary or high school age to counterbalance the general cultural pressures that inundate young people. Many Muslims have become convinced that weekend schools, quranic schools and correspondence courses will never be sufficient to withstand the effects of a secular education, television and other mass media. The goal of establishing Islamic elementary and high schools throughout America is gaining popularity, and many such institutions are already functioning.

Direct da'wah

Open-air preaching

Moving from the sphere of indirect *da'wah* to that of direct confrontation, we find again a variety of current methods. Open-air preaching is the method of choice for some who use Sura 16:125 as their model, a verse which recommends the inviting of people to Islam via "beautiful preaching." However, this method is not common in America. One does not find Muslims arranging the equivalent of Billy Graham crusades at this point. A possible exception would be some of the mass gatherings of the Nation of Islam (i.e., The Million Man March held in Washington, D.C. in 1995), but the purpose and dynamics of such gatherings are quite different from what most Muslim leaders advocate.

Holistic outreach programs

More common at this stage of Muslim activity in America is a holistic program of outreach which concentrates upon specifically defined and limited geographic areas. This type of approach, involving invitations to meetings and seminars, is used by the Islamic Circle of North America and by campus chapters of the Muslim Student Association. They plan and conduct weekly meetings, special "rallies" and study groups dealing with the Qur'an and Islam-related topics. The somewhat exotic reputation that Islam has gained via the modern media, combined with the natural curiosity of young men and women involved in exploring new realms of knowledge, has resulted in well-attended meetings that introduce many to the Muslim campus community.

During its first year, the Islamic Information Center of America (mentioned in the introductory chapter) mailed a form letter to every Protestant church, Catholic church and public school within specifically defined boundaries in the northwest suburbs of Chicago. The letter explained the purpose of the organization and offered to arrange seminars and lectures which would familiarize the members of Christian churches and public school students with Islam. While few churches actually accepted the Center's offer, many high school students made their way to the organization's headquarters to ask questions on the precepts and practices of Islam.

Another invitation to the Christian community was designed to promote dialogue between Christians and Muslims. It stressed the need to join together to pursue goals held in common by both religions, such as "leading people into a pattern of godly living through following the commandments of God and the examples of His Holy Prophets."

Included in the same letter, however, was another objective, one which was much less ecumenical in tone: "We hope to present a clear view of Islam to you and also the Islamic view of Christianity; these dialogues, hopefully, will lead us all to the same Right Path that has been revealed to us through His Chosen Prophets." Reading between the lines, one understands that the ultimate goal of these dialogues was to convince Christians of the truth of Islam and to convert them to the Muslim faith.

Group-oriented activities

The Muslims of America generally discourage door-to-door proselytization of the kind associated with Jehovah's Witnesses and Mormons. Such visitation is considered to invade a person's basic right to privacy and would violate Sura 2:256. In place, however, Muslims throughout America have developed a variety of group-oriented activities. Maryam Jameelah (an American convert to Islam who emigrated to Pakistan after becoming a Muslim) advocates the establishment of small study circles which would allow Muslim women to invite other female friends for discussions.

Summer training camps

The Muslim Student Association sponsors summer training camps which are open to both Muslims and non-Muslims. In addition to the usual activities associated with camping, courses on a number of Islamic subjects are taught.

As mentioned earlier, The Islamic Teaching Center, a division of the Islamic Society of North America, contains a Department of Correctional Facilities. This has proven to be a fruitful field for *da'wah* activity. As early as 1981, this organization was in contact with approximately 4,000 inmates in 310 prisons and had enrolled more than 500 prisoners in an Islamic correspondence course.

Radio and television programming

The use which conservative Christians have made of radio and television in recent decades has not escaped the notice of Muslims. During the late 1970s and early 1980s, plans were made and implemented for Muslim radio and television programming. In 1985 a series entitled "Islam at a Glance" aired in southern California. Programs such as "The Concept of *Shahadah*," "Articles of Faith," "Sirah" and "Aspects of Islamic History" explained to viewers the basic precepts and practices of the Muslim faith.

Literature distribution

There is no doubt, however, that literature distribution is the chief means that Muslims use to share the precepts of their religion. This is in keeping with Islamic tradition, for Muslims have always been "people of the book" (*ahl al-kitab*), emphasizing scholarship and writing to a very large degree. In addition to the above-mentioned Islamic Book Service, sponsored by ISNA, several other major distributors of Islamic materials exist, including Kazi Publications of Chicago, New Era Publications of Ann Arbor, Michigan, and the International Books and Tapes Supply of New York City, to name only a few.

Almost every paramosque organization produces a newsletter, magazine or journal, and many also produce tracts and/or brochures to be used in proselytization efforts. Some have developed educational materials, mostly in the form of small booklets, and a few have published and distributed full-length books, such as Yahiya Emerick's 400-page *What Islam Is All About*.

In addition to academic books which present the Islamic view, the International Institute of Islamic Thought has published a manual authored by Isma'il al-Faruqi entitled *The Islamization of Knowledge: General Principles and Workplan*. This functions as a guide to the production of the textbooks.

The Islamic Information Center of America produces a monthly newsletter called *The Invitation*, and the Islamic Circle of North America publishes a bimonthly entitled *Tehreek*. This latter organization has also established its own publishing arm called the ICNA Book Service and has produced, among several other titles, a *Manual of Da'wah*, which contains instructions for how to distribute pamphlets "at public places: waiting rooms of offices and hospitals, shopping centers, airports and bus stations."

The Muslim Student Association puts out *Al-Ittihad*, one of the leading Islamic serials in America, and has also developed the *Islamic Correspondence Course* and the *Manual for Islamic Weekend and Summer Schools*. Finally, there is the Islamic Society of North America's *Islamic Horizons*, one of the most comprehensive Islamic magazines produced in America.

The above is only a tiny sampling of the literature produced by Muslims in North America. In addition to these, one can order materials from international agencies such as the Islamic Propagation Centre of Durban, South Africa. This Centre's founder and president was Ahmed Deedat, arguably the most famous of the modern Muslim apologists. Deedat's booklets, cassette recordings and videotapes, all of which seek to prove the superiority of Islam over Christianity, have gained a worldwide reputation. During his lifetime, they led to invitations for Deedat to speak and debate in a multitude of countries.

An increasing flurry of activity is occurring as Muslims from coast to coast marshal their resources to take the gospel of Islam to the American people. If the reader has not already encountered a Muslim *da'i* or seen tracts and brochures authored by Muslims, he probably will in the not-too-distant future. But how effective are these methods at producing converts to the Islamic religion? This will be the subject of our next chapter.

Notes

1   Muzammil H. Siddiqui, "Muslims in a Non-Muslim Society," *Islamic Horizons*, May-June 1986, 22.

2   Beshir Adam Rehma, "How to Establish an Islamic Center: A Step-by-Step Approach," in *Let Us Learn: Issues of Your Concern*, ed. Abdel-Hadi Omer (Beloit, WI: Published by the Editor, 1987), 55.

3   Some scholars claim that the Byzantine Empire required a sixteen percent tax from its citizens, while the *jizya*—the tax levied upon non-Muslims residing in a Muslim state—was only about two percent of one's income.

4   There is a great deal of controversy as to how "normal" the lives of *dhimmis* actually were during the period following the conquests. Some historians maintain that Muslims usually fulfilled all of the legal requirements regarding *dhimmis* and that Jews and Christians lived undisturbed lives as second-class citizens. Others hold that in most locations, *dhimmis* were harassed, their property stolen, their families broken apart, their women taken as wives or concubines and their children enslaved. For a detailed exploration of these circumstances, see Bat Ye'or, *The Decline of Eastern Christianity under Islam* (Teaneck, NJ: Fairleigh Dickinson University Press, 1996).

5   For details regarding this as well as other projects, see Robert D. Crane, "Premise and Process in the Islamization of Knowledge: A Contribution Toward Unity in Diversity," in *Preparing to Islamize America: A Research Proposal*, ed. Robert D. Crane (Herndon, VA: International Institute of Islamic Thought, 1987), 10.

3

Converting to Islam

Noted Islamicist John Esposito has written *The Islamic Threat: Myth or Reality?* Newspaper and magazine articles regularly speculate on the future of Islam, its rapid growth and increasing global influence. With the fall of the Iron Curtain and the normalization of relations between the United States and the nations of the former Soviet Union, some have claimed that the Islamic world has become the major opponent of the West.[1]

Occasionally I am asked whether or not I perceive Islam to be a "threat" to the world in general or to Christianity in particular. My answer is always an ambivalent "yes *and* no." Muslims could indeed be considered a threat to certain aspects of the American lifestyle because of their increasing activism in the political, economic and religious spheres of the modern world.

Politically, fundamentalist Muslims—by which we mean those who seek to return Islam to its roots, applying Islamic law and traditions in a literal manner in terms of politics, economics and society—are seeking to consolidate their power and expand their influence both within the "Islamic heartland" (North Africa and the Middle East) and beyond. The competing worldviews of Islam, Christianity, secular democracy and Marxism tear at people in Africa south of the Sahara, particularly along the eastern coast. Muslims have become increasingly vocal in their attempts to persuade Africans that Islam is the only intelligent option.

Within economics, the West has already tasted the power of the world's Muslims in the form of the oil embargos of the 1970s. The monetary policies of such tiny countries as Saudi Arabia can have a significant impact upon global economics.[2] A large percentage of the oil revenues of Muslim nations is being committed to the construction of mosques and Islamic centers in nearly every major city of the world. This makes economics a significant issue from the standpoint of the Christian world mission. Muslims are growing increasingly committed to spreading their faith over the entire planet, and their goal will have profound implications for Christians from both offensive and defensive perspectives.

A case in point: as Islamic "militancy" increases, reports of the repression and even persecution of Christians living in Muslim lands increase as well. This is true even in countries where Muslims and non-Muslims have enjoyed a relatively peaceful coexistence for hundreds of years.

These matters obviously cause concern, no matter where one happens to live. Already comprising at least one-fifth of the world's population and growing faster than any other world religion, the adherents of Islam have the potential of changing the ways in which people relate to each other all over the earth.

A Political Union?

Despite these concerns, there is no cause for a hysterical outcry that "The Muslims are coming! The Muslims are coming!" Some Muslim nations have indeed begun to make their presence known in the international political arena. But these nations are unable to unite into a single bloc which would make them a truly potent force. It is true that when a resolution regarding, for instance, the nation of Israel comes to a vote in the United Nations, Muslim countries nearly always vote together.

But on most other issues, the various Islamic countries tend to look after their own interests. Attempts to forge a political union of Muslim nations, such as the now defunct United Arab Republic, have never succeeded. In general, all of the nations which contain a majority Muslim population have chosen to go their own ways and remain autonomous.

Muslim countries tend to maintain their independence because of the centuries-old preoccupation with national and ethnic distinctives. Arab Muslims differ from Turkish Muslims, who in turn differ from Iranian Muslims, who are distinct from

Indonesian Muslims, and so on. In Islam—as in all other world-class religions—cultural differences contribute significantly to religious factions.

The existence of these factions has led to a great deal of internal dissension within the Muslim world. The Shi'ite Iranians criticize the Sunni Egyptians and the Turks for their "compromises" with Western culture, while the Egyptians and Turks criticize the Iranians and the Libyans for their isolationism and sponsorship of international terrorism. A solution to the disunity and differences is not even a remote possibility in the foreseeable future.

But there are other more positive reasons why Muslims may not be the threat others perceive them to be. While Muslims seem unable to get along with each other, the ability of most Muslim nations to get along with Western nations, particularly with America, has notably improved. While some fundamentalists may still speak of the United States as "The Great Satan," this epithet does not express the views of most Muslims, though many still perceive the West to be secularized and morally decadent.

But recent developments, such as the cooperation between Muslim nations and the United States to halt Iraq's aggression during the Gulf War, broke down many barriers. This situation—in which Muslims allied with Westerners against fellow Muslims—has led to positive changes in perceptions on both sides.

An Economic Union?

Economically, Muslims work together on a much larger scale than in the realm of politics—at least in countries with large reserves of crude oil. The Organization of Petroleum Exporting Countries (OPEC) regularly made headline news throughout the 1970s and even into the early 1980s. During and after the 1973 Arab-Israeli war, oil embargos played a major role in reshaping international economics and politics alike. Predictions of a worldwide scarcity of oil products appeared in such works as Paul and Anne Ehrlich's *The End of Affluence* (1974).

But according to Mark Sagoff, writing recently in *The Atlantic Monthly*, recoverable world reserves of oil have actually *increased* by more than fifty percent since the time of the Ehrlichs' predictions. Sagoff says these reserves currently stand at 1,000 billion barrels. The pretax price of gasoline, he adds, was lower during the 1980s than at any other time since 1947.[3] Such statistics indicate that the Muslim oil threat is not nearly as great as earlier predictions.

A Religious Union?

The religious influence of the Muslim world, however, is much less clear-cut. By its very nature religious power is qualitatively different from either political or economic power. The flexing of political and economic muscle is limited in ways which religious power is not. If a country's political or economic measures threaten neighboring lands, the international community often implements countermeasures to halt or at least mitigate the offending policies. But religious policies are seldom put into the same category as politics and economics. What a country decides with regard to a nationwide religious policy is not considered significant unless it has political or economic ramifications. (An example was the revival of the Shinto religion in Japan, which was largely responsible for the ferocity of Japanese aggression during World War II.)

But a policy which, for instance, has the effect of repressing non-Muslim religious minorities in Muslim countries usually only catches the attention of such organizations as Amnesty International or the occasional newspaper reporter looking for a human interest story. Since religious policies do not affect Americans or Western Europeans the way an oil embargo does, they ignore such policies for the most part. Thus Islam can be a substantial threat to the freedom of religious minorities to practice their beliefs, particularly in Muslim countries.

But what about countries in which Muslims are only a small minority? Could Muslims be considered a threat to the Christian churches of America? Is it true that Muslims are winning converts in such great numbers that they could soon put Christians on the defensive, particularly in the larger cities of the United States? To answer these and related questions, we will examine conversion to Islam for the remainder of this chapter and into the next.

First of all, it is indeed true that some Westerners in America and Europe are converting to the Muslim faith. This has been occurring for a number of years, although the rate has increased in the last two decades. But here we must be careful neither to give nor gain false impressions. One may read that the *percentage* of Islam's growth rate in America is tremendous. But when dealing with comparatively small numbers, a very large percentage increase may still translate into very few individuals. Such is the case with Islam in America. We may state with accuracy that some Americans are converting to Islam, but we are not in danger of being overrun by Muslim converts in the foreseeable future.

Nevertheless, the study of conversion to Islam is fascinating, and the discerning Christian can learn a great deal about both Islam *and* Christianity as a result. Ideas gained from an examination of the "how and why" of conversion to the Muslim faith can greatly aid Christians in their evangelistic endeavors. How is this the case?

Ethnic Muslims

Before discussing this topic, we must distinguish between two of the major Muslim groups residing in America. Just as Christians can be categorized according to their doctrinal beliefs, ritual practices, ethnic or racial background and country of origin, so can Muslims. We may speak first of a group I will term *ethnic Muslims,* which includes the adherents of Islam who have immigrated to America from North African, Eastern European or Middle Eastern countries.

Ethnic Muslims comprise slightly more than half of the American Muslim population. They may be Arabs, Iranians, Iraqis, Lebanese, Palestinians, Egyptians, Turks, Yugoslavians and so on. Those who come from any of these countries bring with them traditions and customs which have characterized their peoples for centuries. In this group we will also include Anglo converts to the Islamic faith. I use the term "Anglo" quite loosely, denoting all converts who do not fit into the classification which follows next.

Muslim Adherents

The other major grouping of Muslims in America is comprised of the African-American adherents of Islam. These persons have formed an indigenous Muslim grouping unique to American society. We will examine this complex movement in detail in chapters 5 through 7. Conversion to African-American Islam is, in several respects, a very different proposition from conversion to the Islam of ethnic Muslims.

Since 1986 I have been collecting the published testimonies and conducting interviews with Anglo-Americans who have converted to the Muslim faith. I have gathered well over 100, and while this is admittedly not a large sampling, it is at least characterized by breadth and depth. The subjects consist of both men and women, and the majority could be characterized as having been "religious" in some sense prior to their conversion to Islam. Some of my sample were Jewish, some considered themselves non-religious, but most claimed to have been Christian. Of these, the majority were either Roman Catholic or Episcopalian. But the collection also includes a number of Baptists, and even a few who considered themselves to have been born again.

The Conversion Experience

Nearly all of the subjects followed a specific sequence in their conversion experience. Most had been raised in typical American homes, attending a church or synagogue on occasion and exhibiting at least some interest in spiritual matters while growing up. Somewhere between the ages of sixteen and twenty, however, they had undergone what might be termed a spiritual crisis. This resulted in a deliberate decision to reject the religious precepts of their upbringing.[4]

A period followed either of moratorium, in which religious interest was more or less suspended, or of religious experimentation, during which several different religious options were explored. Most of my subjects fell in the latter category. They experimented first with Eastern religions, such as various forms of Hinduism (i.e., Hare Krishna) or Buddhism (such as Zen), or they became involved in some of the recent spiritual phenomena commonly labeled the New Age Movement.

All of these religious systems appear exciting and exotic, in many ways radically different from the mainstream religions of America. Participation in Eastern faiths often has the flavor of rebellion, which from a psychological point of view is highly significant. Many young people desire to rebel to some degree against their parents and society, mainly to establish their own identity. One of the most satisfying ways of doing this is to choose a religious practice utterly at variance with that of their parents. This is made easier when Christianity seems to be out-of-date, much like their parents' values and ethics. The combined thrill of the new, the exotic and rebellion makes the new faith seem like the perfect means of fulfillment.

But the thrill usually vanishes quickly. According to studies conducted by noted sociologists of religion, the average length of time a Westerner remains within an Eastern religious faith is slightly less than two years. As one gains greater familiarity with the new religion, the philosophical and theological ideas at its base often turn out to be incomprehensible or unacceptable.

The individual becomes increasingly dissatisfied, begins to raise objections, meets with ostracism from the firmly committed and finally leaves the group altogether. Almost always, another period of "seeking" begins. Most people have no intention of returning to the Christianity they were raised to follow. Doing so would acknowledge that Dad and Mom were correct after all.

The average amount of time spent on the seeker's journey is fourteen years, until the person reaches the late twenties or early thirties. This is the point when contact with Islam or with individual Muslims produces results. Due to its content and origin, Islam offers a middle road between Christianity or Judaism and a faith with Eastern roots. Islam has enough of the exotic that one need not be concerned about "giving in" to parental or cultural pressure. Due to the media's portrayal of the Muslim faith, a person can be satisfied that he is converting to a belief system very much at odds with the surrounding culture.

But at the same time, Islam does have much in common with Christianity and Judaism. The Muslim faith returns the convert to many of the Sunday school characters of youth: Adam and Eve, Noah, Abraham, Moses, David, Jesus and others. The convert finds in the Qur'an familiar stories such as the creation account and Joseph with Potiphar's wife. These narratives are altered from the biblical accounts, but they are still recognizable. The familiarity of the old together with the newly exotic make the religion an ideal middle ground. Many choose the faith precisely for this reason.

In the next chapter we will look at five specific characteristics of Islam which make that religion so attractive to many Americans.

Notes

1   See, for instance, George Otis, Jr., *The Last of the Giants: Lifting the Veil on Islam and the End-Times* (Grand Rapids, MI: Chosen Books, 1991).

2   For an interesting scenario of the effect that "petroleum politics" could potentially have on the world, see Paul E. Erdman's novel *The Crash of '79* (New York, NY: Simon and Schuster, 1976).

3   Mark Sagoff, "Do We Consume Too Much?" *The Atlantic Monthly,* June 1997, 83.

4   The years mentioned here (sixteen to twenty) are highly significant from the standpoint of the spiritual life. It is during these years that the overwhelming majority of decisions are made either to commit one's life to Christ and to follow the precepts of His Word, or to reject Christianity completely. For more details, see Larry Poston, "The Adult Gospel," *Christianity Today,* September 1990, 23-25.

4

Islam's Appeal

In my research of Anglo-Americans who have converted to Islam, I have found that there are five
characteristics of the religion which appealed to
nearly all of them. Yet each of these characteristics
is either also found in Christianity or not actually
true of Islam.

1. Simplicity

What Muslims say

Converts usually admire Islam for its simplicity. For
the person on the street, Islam does not appear to be
nearly as complicated as Christianity. Apart from the
larger Roman Catholic and Orthodox divisions, literally tens of thousands of Protestant denominations
and sects claim to convey spiritual truth. Among this
bewildering array, one finds theological distinctions
between Calvinism and Arminianism, premillen-
nialism and amillennialism, and the baptism of infants

and the baptism of adults, to name only a few. How can an outsider possibly choose between all the various options available?

In Islam, such distinctions do not appear to exist. This perception is entirely wrong, for the Muslim religion actually contains many variations. But this is precisely the point: the vast majority of Americans know so little about Islam that it appears to be much simpler than it is. And Muslims market their faith accordingly. The *single* requirement for becoming a Muslim is to pronounce the *Shahada* before a group of Muslim elders.

What Christians say

But Muslims are not nearly as united as they might appear to be. Only one major division is within the religion—the separation between the Sunnis and the Shi'ites. But each of these spheres of Islam has literally hundreds of smaller divisions, and few Americans are aware of them. These separations have occurred from the beginning of Islamic history. One can speak of the four separate schools of law which developed in the early centuries among the Sunni Muslims: the Malaki, Hanafi, Shafi'i and Hanbali schools. Among the Shi'ites, divisions occurred over the identity of the successors to Ali: the Fivers, the Seveners and the Twelvers.

Then there is Sufi Islam, which we have characterized as "mystical Islam." The Sufis tended to divide into various schools or orders (*tariqas*) which were organized around specific individuals, usually known as *shaykhs*. These orders multiplied and subdivided through the centuries.

And among the peoples of North Africa there has arisen a phenomenon known as folk Islam, which intermingles the beliefs and practices of classical Islam with indigenous animistic religions. The practice of folk Islam has resulted in a number of interesting groups, each giving allegiance to a *marabout*, a leader having political authority who also is endowed with special spiritual power known as *baraka*.

Adherents of Islam have struggled for centuries to manage the enormous diversity that exists within the Muslim world and, in reality, have succeeded no better than have Christians.

What Muslims say

Adding to the "simple" appeal of orthodox Islam is the fact that the ritualistic practices of the religion—the five daily prayers, charitable giving, fasting during Ramadan and making the pilgrimage to Mecca—are not required to attain salvation, though they are not exactly optional. Many Muslims participate in these practices only occasionally or not at all, and are still in most cases considered to be Muslims. It is recommended that converts learn the Arabic language, abstain from eating pork products and attend the Friday afternoon prayer service at a mosque—but none of these things are absolutely required to retain one's Islamicity.

Islam is also portrayed as exemplifying simplicity. The religion holds that every Muslim should seek to emulate Muhammad's lifestyle in all respects, and his life was exceedingly simple. He did not seek riches. He never lived in a palace or owned herds of horses or camels, and he did not maintain an extensive wardrobe, fine jewelry or other trappings. Instead, he ate simply, lived in the humblest of dwellings and wore plain, everyday clothing. Muslims often contrast their prophet's lifestyle with the extravagances of the Roman Catholic clergy. The ornate clothing and ornaments of the pope and other officials are easy targets. The flashy proponents of the "health and wealth gospel" found within certain spheres of Protestantism have come in for criticism as well.

These observations are significant, for psychologists and sociologists have noted that spiritual seekers usually expect religious leaders to live somewhat austere, simplistic lives as a mark of their "holiness." Wealth and materialism, on the other hand, are a sign of worldliness, no matter how many Scripture passages are quoted that say God's favor is shown through the acquisition of wealth. Thus for many American observers, Islam appears to have maintained a "holier" standard than Christianity. This has lent credibility that is sadly lacking in many sectors of Christendom today.

What Christians say

It is true that in many respects Muhammad led an exemplary life. From all accounts he was unaffected by materialistic desires. In his choice of dwelling, diet, clothing and personal possessions, he was a simple, humble man. Some Christians have criticized him for his polygamous marriages, for according to tradition he took eleven wives after the death of his first wife. But this objection is difficult to sustain in light of the

Bible's accounts of the polygamy of such notables as Jacob, David and Solomon. And the Mosaic Covenant makes allowances for polygamous relationships (such as Deuteronomy 21:15). There is little merit to bringing up this issue with Muslims.

Muhammad's life of simplicity may have been exemplary when compared to the gaudiness and pomposity of the Roman Catholic and Eastern Orthodox clergy. But even a casual study of Islamic history will reveal that few of his successors took his example to heart. The *caliphs* and leading ministers of the Muslim world lived in an exotic splendor that rivaled or exceeded the Christian religious officials. The opulence gained from the booty of conquests and taxes levied upon non-Muslims produced extravagant lifestyles. The Mogul Empire of India, for instance, produced at its height the Taj Mahal—a structure very different from the rugged tents which housed Muhammad and his family.

This brief perusal of Islamic history is not meant to critique Muslim policies; it intends to show that in the area of material simplicity, the distinction between Islam and Christianity is not as great as is often claimed. Indeed, one could with comparative ease make the case that *biblical* Christianity is actually much simpler in essence than quranic Islam. Muslims claim that a formal proclamation of the *Shahada* is all that is required for one to become a Muslim. But to be accounted righteous on the Day of Judgment, one must live a life in which one's good deeds outweigh the bad.

However, in a letter to the Romans, the Apostle Paul proclaimed that the essential message of the

Christian faith is the need to acknowledge Jesus as Lord of one's life and live in the light of His resurrection (Romans 10:9-10). Humble acknowledgment that Jesus is Lord and Master of one's life coupled with a dynamic belief that He is a risen and thus living Lord are the sole requirements that God, in His graciousness, has for the salvation of human beings. The new birth and adoption into the family of God are processes which cannot be earned or merited in any way by any person. In its essence, biblical Christianity is extraordinarily simplistic. It is unfortunate that persons who have clearly never understood the radical simplicity of God's grace have made it so complicated.

The Gospel accounts make it clear that in many ways the life of Jesus was even simpler than that of Muhammad. Muhammad had at least a place where he could "lay his head"; Jesus stated that He had no such place. His itinerant ministry kept Him constantly on the move. Muhammad was surrounded by his wives and children. Jesus, on the other hand, lived much more austerely. He chose to forgo marriage and family to devote Himself single-mindedly to the instruction and training of His disciples. In these ways, and in many others, the life of Jesus was at least as simple as that of Muhammad.

2. Rationality

What Muslims say

Secondly, Islam claims to be a more rational faith than Christianity, which is said to contain irrational beliefs and practices. Concepts such as the Trinity and the substitutionary atonement of Christ through His death by crucifixion are held up as incomprehensible and nonsensical distortions of Jesus' teachings.

The difficulty of explaining the Trinitarian doctrine—that God is One and yet is Three simultaneously—lends credibility to the conviction that Christians are "blind believers"; because of tradition, they have never questioned whether their doctrines or practices make sense. Muslims use the teaching that Jesus is the Son of God as an example of irresponsible belief on the part of Christians, as the Qur'an states in Sura 18:4-5 that such an idea is blasphemy.

In other words, Muslims maintain that the early Christians did not say that God had a son and that Jesus did not claim to be the Son of God. Christians today believe this fallacy only because someone invented the idea and passed it down as truth. Another disputed teaching is Jesus' sacrifice as an atonement for human sin. According to Islam, this is clearly incorrect. For the Qur'an states that no one can "bear the burdens of another" (see Suras 39:7 and 53:38).

The Muslim faith, on the other hand, is "the thinking person's religion." Its teachings are black and white, Muslims claim, containing no irrational concepts to confuse and no miracles to explain. Muhammad was just a man—a Prophet of God, according to Muslim belief, but a man nonetheless. His words were the revelation of God, and thus completely understandable and logical. Christians will forever apologize for the actions of the Church against such men as Galileo, who taught the Copernican theory that the earth revolves around the sun.

But Muslims claim that the teachings of the Qur'an will never embarrass them, for they coincide precisely with modern science and the "natural" thoughts and feelings of all human beings. The adherents of Islam like to quote Maurice Bucaille's book *The Bible, The Qur'an and Science*, in which the author claims that the Qur'an could not have been the work of a mere human being.[1]

What Christians say

It is true that Christianity contains some doctrinal beliefs that are difficult to explain from the standpoint of philosophical rationalism. The doctrine of the Trinity has always been problematic. When attempting to explain it, one is forced to use words and concepts which never quite communicate what is essentially a mystery. But the problem is not so much with the rationality of the Christian faith as it is with the shortcomings of human thought and language to conceptualize God. To say that God's Oneness consists of a divine Threeness communicates as best we can the essence of God's being.

But such an expression does not easily fit into the human parameters of what we call "rational." Muslims (and others as well) assume that Oneness cannot consist of Threeness. But the reasoning behind this assumption is itself not necessarily "rational." The generally accepted idea is that God is a wholly self-existent and eternal Being who transcends humanity and the rest of the created order. Would it not be reasonable to assume that God's Oneness very possibly—even *probably*—exceeds the ideas of finite human beings?

The same would hold true for the incarnation of God in Jesus, His substitutionary atonement for the sins of mankind through His death by crucifixion, and the miracles He performed during His life on earth. There is no reason to discard any Christian doctrinal belief if one starts from the presupposition that God is by definition a transcendent, omnipotent, omniscient, omnipresent and autonomous Being. Such a Being is indeed able to exceed human ideas of oneness, incarnate Himself in human flesh, atone for the sins of His own created order and transcend the laws of that creation.

The Qur'an specifically denies each of these Christian doctrines. More knowledgeable Muslim theologians, then, do not object to Christianity because of the alleged philosophical irrationality of Christian beliefs; they object, rather, because what they believe to be the revelation of God (the Qur'an) denies their legitimacy entirely. This is the most significant difference between Christianity and Islam. Christians claim that the Bible is the inspired Word of God and the receptacle of all spiritual truth, whereas Muslims claim that the Qur'an holds this position.

For the sake of argument, let us accept Islam's claim to be superior to Christianity because of Christianity's "irrational" doctrines and acceptance of miraculous occurrences. Is the religion of Islam so much more "rational" with regard to its own beliefs and practices?

Muslims hold strongly the idea of divine predestination; indeed, classical Islam could be said to be more "Calvinistic" than Reformed Christianity in the area of soteriology. The attempts by Muslim scholars to meld the sovereignty of God and the responsibility of human beings has led to many interesting debates through the centuries, including one which produced the scholar Al-Ashari's "doctrine of acquisition."

This doctrine is held as orthodox but does not fit at all within the bounds of rational thought. Al-Ashari's attempt to combine God's sovereignty and human responsibility led him to state that God creates all acts—both good and evil—but human beings "acquire" or perform them. God is thus not responsible because He does not "force" anyone to perform sinful acts. He may, however, be said to create them. Most Western philosophers find problems with the logic of this teaching which most Muslims accept unquestioningly.

The doctrine of the "uncreatedness" of the Qur'an states that the Qur'an as the Word of Allah is eternally existent. The Qur'an is never held to be "God," of course, yet it is said to be eternally existent, with no beginning and no end, a prerogative which belongs only to God. Muslims explain how the Qur'an can be eternal and not be "God," of course. But these explanations do not fit within the bounds of "rational thought" any better than Christian explanations of the Trinity.

With regard to miracles, the Qur'an accepts many found in the Bible and presents them as truth—even some recorded in non-canonical writings rather than the canon itself. (One is the account of Jesus fashioning dirt and clay into birds and breathing life into them.) In addition, Muslims believe the traditional narrative of the "Night Journey of Muhammad," in which the prophet is transported on horseback into the very presence of God Himself as factual. But this is certainly a miraculous event, easily placed in the same category as the miracles of Jesus. Several "irrational" events occur within the Islamic faith—without perturbing Muslims. Why, then, should the aspects of Christianity which are difficult to explain trouble them?

3. "This-worldliness"

What Muslims say

Thirdly, Islam may be characterized as a "this-worldly religion." The Qur'an is said to contain a prescription for an ideal political, economic, judicial, social, moral and religious system, revealed by God for the benefit of His people. Most Muslims will admit that they have had a great deal of difficulty in agreeing on what this package should look like in real life.

But nearly all believe that such a system is indeed contained in the pages of the Qur'an, and once implemented, will provide the framework for a perfect world order. The Qur'an itself would serve as the charter document for such a "Kingdom of Islam"; this is already the case in such countries as Saudi Arabia, where the constitution is simply the Muslim Scriptures. Islamic law is held to be all-encompassing, addressing every conceivable human issue. Muslims

believe that consistent application of this law will produce a true "peace on earth."

Christians, on the other hand, have struggled
since the earliest days of the faith with the institutional forms of their religious beliefs. It is difficult to
claim that Jesus taught His followers a particular
system of politics, economics or law which could be
labeled Christian. Muslims often ask why the New
Testament contains no information in these areas.
Christians, it is said, are so busy thinking about the
rapture of the Church, the second coming of Jesus
and an afterlife in heaven that they do not concern
themselves with life on earth.

Muslims claim that their faith speaks of *both*; it
gives a plan for institutional structures which will
uphold spiritual principles in the physical world and
at the same time speaks about eternal life in the
hereafter—which will be determined by the actions
one performs in the here and now. Muslims believe
that since they have instructions regarding their
conduct in the present life *and* the life to come, Islam is superior to Christianity.

What Christians say

Is Christianity purely an "other-worldly" faith
with no instructions for how to live in the here and
now? Does Islam actually offer a superior package
to help one live in the present world? It is admittedly
difficult to find evidence that Jesus left His followers a concrete plan for a physical kingdom of heaven
on earth. To the contrary, He told His disciples that
the kingdom was an internal rather than an external
reality (Luke 17:20-21). The kingdom of heaven

is—at least for the time being—an underground kingdom carried within the hearts and minds of its citizens. It is not synonymous with the institutional church, and it does not involve a revival of the patterns of Old Testament Israel—although these and similar errors have been made throughout the history of Christianity.

The chief problems with these ideas are: What would such a "kingdom" actually look like? What form would a Christian political system take? Economic system? Judicial system? Did Jesus advocate a democratic form of government or, since He is the "king," does the Bible support a monarchy? Is individualistic, free enterprise capitalism the Christian economic system? Or is socialism better? Would Jesus favor trial by jury? Capital punishment? In biblical revelation, He took no sides on such issues. He taught that Christians are to live in a manner consistent with the ethical principles of the internal and personal kingdom of God *regardless* of the political, economic or social systems in which they find themselves.

The New Testament expectation that Jesus could return to earth within a short period of time uniquely influences the goals and objectives of Christian men and women. Many regard human institutions as essentially unimportant and not worth the time and energy necessary to change them. They believe that true spiritual transformation only occurs as an internal and personal work of God within individuals. This renders the task of imposing large-scale change via human institutions as mainly useless.

The New Testament does not teach, however, that Christians should never seek to influence the surrounding social environment. But one finds a decidedly different focus than that of institution-oriented Islam. Christians committed to a biblical paradigm seek to transform their surroundings through *internal* change in individuals who together constitute a social environment. Educating an individual regarding the essential gospel message *may* achieve that person's spiritual rebirth, if he responds to the gospel. After regeneration comes the discipleship process, when newly reborn Christians are instructed concerning "everything that Jesus taught" (see Matthew 28:19-20). This should produce in each such individual a biblical worldview.

If enough persons acquire such a worldview in a specific location, or if the regenerated persons occupy influential positions, social environments *may* be changed. There is no guarantee that society at large, which according to Jesus will always consist of a majority of non-Christians (see Matthew 7:13-14), will change. If by God's grace such large-scale changes do occur, they should never be looked upon as establishment of "the kingdom of heaven." But regeneration indeed changes individuals, and even single individuals can have enormous influence in the lives of people through service and ministry. *This* is the "this-worldly" contribution of Christianity, according to the teachings of the New Testament.

From the standpoint of Muslims, the task of creating a literal kingdom of Islam—a "this-worldly" political realm—has not been as clear-cut as some would seem to indicate. Muslims will sometimes speak of the unity which prevailed when the Muslim world was presided over by a *caliph,* a ruler who was to represent the ways of God and exemplify the teachings of Muhammad. In many ways analogous to the Roman Catholic Papacy, the *Caliphate* existed from Muhammad's death until 1924. Thus Muslims claim that for the majority of Islamic history, the kingdom of Islam was a reality because the precepts of Islamic law united Muslim peoples into a cohesive unit.

The claim, however, is highly questionable. At the beginning of the Muslim era, several groups split off from the main body. They refused to recognize the system for choosing Muhammad's successors and showed open disdain for the men selected as the first *caliphs.* The Shi'ites and the Kharijites were two of the most significant offshoots. Throughout Islamic history the Shi'ites have followed their own path and produced their own leaders, although none of the various groups have recognized more than twelve specially anointed *imams*; some only recognize seven, others five.

For those who claim twelve, tradition has it that the twelfth *imam* disappeared, and the Shi'ite Twelvers await his reappearance. Thus their concept of an Islamic kingdom is more in keeping with biblical Christianity: a physical kingdom will not become a reality during the present time. Thus the kingdom of the Shi'ites is much more like that of the New Testament—an invisible kingdom, presided over by an invisible leader. We can see that there is certainly no consensus regarding a "this-worldly package" among Muslims of the world.

The majority of the adherents of Islam followed the Sunni path. The first four *caliphs,* who presided over the Muslim world from A.D. 632 to 661, were considered to be specially empowered. They were given a collective name: the *rashidun,* or "rightly guided ones." During their reign, the expansion of Islam began and the Qur'an was collected. But following these twenty-nine years, the situation quickly deteriorated into power struggles among Arab tribes. Power changed hands from the tribe of Quraysh, to which Muhammad had belonged, to the tribes of the Ummayads and the Abbasids.

Following the chaos wrought by the Mongol invasions, an obscure group of Turkish Muslims, the Ottomans, took power. In other parts of the Muslim world (Egypt and India, for instance), indigenous leaders arose. The last Ottoman *caliph* was deposed in 1924 by Mustafa Kemal Ataturk, who established the modern nation-state called Turkey. Today the Muslim world is broken into several nation-states, and attempts to rebuild a unifying structure have failed.

Added to political disunity, theological strife has plagued Muslims for centuries. The adherents of Islam have had their own "liberal versus conservative" debates, which still are ongoing. The fundamentalist phenomenon, which appears so often in the news media, attempts to return Islam to conservativism. Fundamentalist Muslims desire to do away with philosophical and religious ideas which have been added to Muhammad's original teach-

ings and thus turn the clock back to a less complicated—and purer—way of life.

Another influential group, however, desires to
"modernize" the faith. They chafe under the common stereotype of Islam as medieval and irrelevant
to contemporary humanity. This group believes that
the decision to abandon the liberal arts and sciences
after the Mongol invasions was one of the greatest
mistakes ever made by the Muslim world. In order
to win converts and resume worldwide expansion,
the Muslim faith must appeal to contemporary society.

It should be obvious that the "Islamdom" advo-
cated by the fundamentalists differs radically from
that of modernists. Thus we find that Islam's claim
to offer a unifying package for political, economic,
social and moral aspects of life is spurious. A global
"kingdom of Islam" has never existed, and there is
little chance that it will in the foreseeable future.

4. Equality

What Muslims say

Fourthly, Islam is attractive because it appears to
emphasize the equality of all individuals, races, ethnic groups and social classes. Muslims like to point
to the pilgrimage (*hajj*) ceremony as an illustration
of their commitment to diversity. At the entrance to
the great square in Mecca, in which stands the
Ka'ba, the main shrine of Islam, all Muslims, regardless of race, ethnic background or gender, are
given the same simple clothing to wear for circling
the shrine. These garments become an outward tes-

timony of the equality of all Muslims. Black and White, rich and poor, male and female—all meet in the great square and in unison perform the pilgrimage rituals.

Islam claims to have resolved the problems of race and gender in ways that Christians have been unable to accomplish. History informs us that it was Christians who enslaved Black Africans—many of whom were Muslims—and transported them to America and other parts of the world. And Muslims are well aware that the Christians' Sunday morning worship is perhaps the most segregated event on the North American continent.

Not only does Christianity suffer from racial problems, say Muslims, but from gender problems as well. Christianity teaches that women are subordinate to men and "weaker vessels," while Islam allegedly upholds the full equality of male and female. Muhammad is often presented as the great "liberator" of women on earth.

Many females convert to Islam in reaction to the feminist subculture which formerly held them. A large number of women I have talked to in my research came to believe that the feminist agenda of achieving equality with males was a dead-end street. These converts felt that their drive to compete with men in business, academia, athletics and the like had erased their identity. They no longer understood what it meant to be feminine. The stereotypical Islamic view of women as one of subordination and subjection takes on different overtones in light of the burnout of some American females.

Islam makes a clear distinction between men and women; beyond this the female's status is subject to differing interpretations. Where the feminist sees subordination and degradation, the ex-feminist engaged in a personal search for identity sees respect and protection. While Islam idealizes the role relationships of men and women, some seekers perceive that it places the woman upon a pedestal; she is treasured and wears the traditional Islamic garb as a means of protecting her from the unbridled lusts of heathen men. Islam celebrates the bearing of children, and family values appear to be extremely important.

Consequently, some American females have professed Islam in order to regain a sense of what it means to be truly female. In many cases these women come from "Christian" backgrounds. They say that they did not consider Christianity because of the progress feminism has made within American churches.[2]

What Christians say

The claim that Muslims are without prejudice has been greatly exaggerated. At the beginning of the Islamic period, Arab Muslims considered themselves superior to all other groups who converted to Islam. A non-Arab convert was required to have an Arab sponsor in order to be accepted fully into the faith. One can occasionally still find rhetoric indicating that coming from the Middle East, the heartland of Islam, imparts a slight superiority over those who come from the fringes of the Muslim world.

And it goes without saying that Sunnis are often greatly prejudiced against Shi'ites and vice versa. Bias also exists by many Sunnis against those who follow a Sufi orientation to the faith. And just as there exist Christian cults, groups calling themselves "Christian" that do not subscribe to all orthodox doctrines or practices, Muslims also look upon certain splinter groups, such as the Ahmadiyya and the Ba'hai, as heretical.

Attempts to paint Christians as the original slave masters is hypocritical. The original *jihads* produced an entire class of slaves, as women and children in particular became part of the "booty" acquired by Muslim conquerors. In Egypt, slaves became known as *mamluks*, literally "owned ones." And when the *mamluks* became the ruling class of Egypt, they formed a slave class to serve them.

During the colonial era of the West, Muslims were involved in both the capture and sale of Africans to the slave traders of Europe and America, despite the fact that many of the Africans bore Muslim names and were most likely converts. And reports continue to surface today from organizations like Amnesty International that slave trading is still conducted in Mauritania and the Sudan, Muslim countries in North Africa.

Muslims sensitive to this issue object, saying that slave trading is not in accord with quranic teaching and that those who participate are not really "Muslims." But Christians use this same argument about colonial "Christianity." The Bible very clearly lists "slave traders" among those labeled "lawbreakers and rebels, the ungodly and sinful, the unholy and irreligious" (see 1 Timothy 1:9-10). Christians may with justification claim that those who were involved in such activities were clearly either disobedient or not Christians at all. Due to the efforts of churchmen such as William Wilberforce, a member of the British Parliament, the practice of slavery was outlawed in the British Empire.

Admittedly there still are problems within Christendom regarding racial and ethnic relations. But these problems are due to ignorance, disobedience or immaturity, all of which characterize a great number of those who call themselves Christians. The difficulties do not, therefore, result from any fault intrinsic to the faith itself. Besides the condemnation of slave trading mentioned above, one also finds in the Bible a celebration of diversity within the Church (see 1 Corinthians 12). Scripture portrays the body of Christ as being comprised of "a great multitude that no one could count, from every nation, tribe, people and language" (Revelation 7:9). In Christ, says Paul, "there is neither Jew nor Greek, slave nor free, male nor female" (Galatians 3:28). While Christianity has difficulties in this area, so do Muslims. They have no advantage over Christians when the complete picture is seen.

With regard to gender issues, we are again faced with a rather complex situation. Christians have been struggling for a long time with the tension presented in the New Testament regarding the role of women. On the one hand, as we have noted, Paul claims that in Christ there is neither male nor female (Galatians 3:28), implying equality between the two. But Paul also states that wives are to "submit to their husbands in everything" (Ephesians 5:24) and forbids a woman to "teach or have authority over a man" (1 Timothy 2:12).

Rather than attempting to resolve these two streams of thought, Christian groups have usually chosen to follow one emphasis or the other. Muslims have therefore targeted both emphases. They castigate Christians who teach the subordination of women to men for denying women their rights as human beings created by Allah. At the same time, they criticize Christians who appoint women to positions of leadership in the church for failing to recognize the distinctions between males and females ordained by Allah. Islam is presented as offering a perfectly balanced view of the issue.

But a closer examination reveals that in actuality, Muslims are faced with the same problems as Christians. The Qur'an demonstrates the same ambivalence toward the role of women as the Bible. In Sura 4:34, for instance, righteous women are permitted in their husband's absence to "guard whatever Allah would have them guard," implying an equality of status. In the very same verse, however, men are given responsibility to be the protectors of women since men are stronger, and receive permission to "beat lightly" those who do not conduct themselves properly.

It is true that from the standpoint of the seventh century, Muhammad did indeed improve the lot of women in the Middle East. But this was a very relative improvement. From being eligible to receive no inheritance at all from the death of her husband, the Middle Eastern wife became eligible to inherit a third of his property (the children received the remainder). From having no say in legal matters whatsoever, the testimony of two women became equal to that of one man. And from having to share a man with numerous other wives, she would now have to share a husband with no more than three (since the Qur'an limits polygamous marriages to a maximum of four wives).

Thus it may be said that "Islam champions the rights of women." But from the perspective of the twenty-first century, none of the above examples would be even closely indicative of "equality." Consequently, Islam has its feminists as well, one of the most notable being Taslima Nasrin, a Bangladeshi author currently in hiding in Stockholm because of death threats issued against her by Muslim fundamentalists. We can see that, as with matters of race and ethnicity, Muslims have no advantages over Christians with respect to gender issues.

5. Individualism

What Muslims say

Finally, Islam is perceived as being a do-it-yourself religion. Muslims do not have a strongly developed hierarchical structure, such as in Roman Catholicism, Eastern Orthodoxy and some Protestant denominations. A mosque may have an *imam*, or prayer leader, who in some circles is beginning to function more and more like a Protestant pastor, but historically this has not been the case. The *imam* has simply been the leader for the prayer times during the day.

In traditional Islam there are no priests, no mediators between God and human beings. It is highly personalized and individualistic, and the rituals may be performed in the privacy of one's own home. Membership or attendance of a mosque is not required, and there is no stigma attached to visiting a mosque only once or twice a year during the festival seasons (the *Eid al-Adha*, which brings to a close the season of the *hajj*, or pilgrimage, and the *Eid al-Fitr*, which marks the end of the Ramadan fasting period).

In contrast, Christianity is rife with mediators. The New Testament teaching says that Jesus is the ultimate Mediator between God and human beings (1 Timothy 2:5), but history has added others. The hierarchy of the Roman Catholic Church has the pope, cardinals, archbishops, bishops and priests as mediators. Many Catholics pray to Mary, the mother of Jesus. Hundreds of canonized saints are believed to provide aid in times of spiritual and physical troubles. Many modern Americans find this too complex a structure.

This hierarchy and its medieval superstitions carry all the negative connotations of the 1960s' "establishment." In contrast, Islam's individuality and voluntary aspects appeal to young Americans, who are highly individual in spiritual matters and who do not like the restrictions of ritualized worship. Islam lends itself very well to contemporary American thinking.

What Christians say

Is Islam a "do-it-yourself" religion requiring no mediators between humans and the divine? Muslims can claim advantages here only over certain forms of Christianity. It is true that Roman Catholicism, Eastern Orthodoxy and some high-church Protestant denominations maintain a pronounced distinction between clergy and laity. In many cases members of the clerical class allegedly have power and authority to function as mediators between God and ordinary persons.

This innovation in Christian doctrine and praxis is highly unfortunate. The Bible does describe a system of leadership and authority in the Church of God, consisting of elders and deacons/deaconesses (see 1 Timothy 3). But Jesus abolished the concepts of human mediation and priesthood when He assumed these roles. Jesus is the sole Mediator between God and human beings, says Paul (1 Timothy 2:5). Human mediators no longer *exist* between Christians and God; each person is a "priest" for himself (1 Peter 2:9).

The Roman Catholic Church retrieved the institution of the priesthood largely from the Old Testament Mosaic Covenant. This was an unjustified action without a trace of New Testament support. Historically, it preserved immaturity and ignorance on the part of many who were truly Christian in the biblical sense of the word. It has contributed as well to the nominality and falsity of a great deal of what passes for Christianity in the world today. Tragically Muslim rhetoric is often closer to New Testament precepts in this area than is Christian practice.

But here again we have mostly rhetoric. For in many parts of the Islamic world, the same phenomenon occurred as it did in Christian history. The concept of human mediation came into the Muslim faith without warrant from either the Qur'an or tradition. Many North African Muslims look to their tribal *shaykhs* as mediators who possess special powers to ward off sicknesses and other problems.

Certainly the early *imams* within Shi'ite Islam, and even their modern successors, such as the *ayatollahs* of Iran, are in the minds of the masses endowed with a much more exalted status than a simple prayer leader. Chaos reigned during the funeral cortege of the Ayatollah Khomeini. So many people sought to touch his body to gain some of his *baraka* (spiritual blessing or power) that his corpse toppled off of its bier. This is an example of what will most likely continue among Muslim peoples from lesser-developed nations.

In America, of course, the situation is different from Iran. But one may question how Islam is a do-it-yourself faith for new converts, particularly those from an Anglo background. In some cases these persons have gained almost celebrity status, showcased by Muslims anxious to demonstrate that their religion is not limited to persons from Middle Eastern or African backgrounds. The musician formerly known as Cat Stevens (now Yusuf Islam) is an example of this phenomenon.

A convert will likely not admit that he is being pushed into the limelight and forced to study Islam and Arabic, to attend a mosque and to speak often about his conversion. But close acquaintances with several such persons reveal that this is indeed the case. To join a fellowship with other believers who form an accountability structure is, of course, advisable. But to claim that one's new faith allows more personal autonomy than does Christianity is highly inaccurate.

Do Christians Measure Up?

These five characteristics of the Muslim faith appear to be the most attractive, although a variety of other items have caught the attention of Americans. Some are impressed by the conservative morality which characterizes many Muslims; as a rule the adherents of Islam oppose abortion, homosexuality, sexual promiscuity and feminism. They favor strict sentences for criminals, including the death penalty for capital crimes. To prospective and new converts, Christians appear to have compromised their beliefs on these issues and become weak and cowardly, and Muslims have taken up the banner they let fall.

Close examination finds, however, that Islam's most attractive aspects are not actually superior to Christianity. Characteristics mentioned by converts to Islam as representing distinct advantages over the Christian faith actually first appeared in the Bible. In most cases, these items do not exist in Islam in the way or to the extent claimed.

As Christians, we can learn several things from these observations. First, whether we like to admit it or not, *appearance* is much more important than *reality* in public relations. Islam *appears* to be superior to Christianity in several ways—although in actuality it is superior in none of these. And Christianity *appears* to be irrelevant, "medieval" and unfit for a sophisticated modern American, whereas in reality *biblical* Christianity will meet every need of any individual.

To counteract this public image, we as evangelicals must work on our appearance—not by putting on a show or presenting a facade. But we must learn to emphasize certain aspects of the Bible's teaching in a way that reaches persons within our society that Muslims are attracting. We must show that:

- Christianity is indeed essentially simple and reasonable—as long as we do not impose strictly human ideas of rationality upon it.

- The Bible offers a holistic approach to life. In discipling others, we must teach about all of life, not just the "spiritual."

- Our Scriptures celebrate diversity and prohibit prejudice of all kinds.

- And finally, in accordance with the Protestant Reformers' biblical doctrine of "the priesthood of all believers," Christianity is the ultimate do-it-yourself system of faith and practice.

Make no mistake. When individuals apprehend Christianity in its New Testament form, and when they understand the claims of Islam as merely unfulfilled human aspirations, they will embrace the former.

Notes

1 Maurice Bucaille, *The Bible, The Qur'an and Science* (Paris: Segher, 1987), 163.
2 For more information about this topic, see Carol Anway's *Daughters of Another Path* (Lee's Summit, MO: Yawna Publications, 1995). The author's daughter is a convert from Christianity to Islam.

2

African-American Islam

5

Elijah Muhammad and the Nation of Islam

Many older Americans vividly recall the boxing career of Cassius Clay, the African-American fighter who defeated Sonny Liston to win the World Heavyweight Championship in 1964. Clay's flamboyance and braggadocio gained him notoriety. Then, immediately after acquiring his championship title, he joined the Black Muslim movement and changed his name to Muhammad Ali. This was the first time some Americans were exposed to this movement, but not the last. The next year, Black Muslims were again in the headlines when the man known as Malcolm X was assassinated in New York City's Harlem district.

Today, some thirty-five years later, many African-American sports figures have adopted Muslim names, and a best-selling autobiography and a major motion picture have told the story of Malcolm X.

In addition, Louis Farrakhan, leader of the Nation of Islam, regularly captures headlines. His sponsorship of the Million Man March in Washington, D.C. in 1995 kept the Black Muslim movement at the forefront of the American scene. Who are the "Black Muslims," and what relationship do they have to ethnic Islam? The story is complex, and we will need to turn back the pages of history to the early 1930s in Detroit, Michigan.

The year 1930 was singularly difficult for many persons in America. The Depression of 1929 stripped them of employment and dignity. African-Americans were faced with a particularly bad plight. Later in the nineteenth century and early during the twentieth, hundreds of Black families had migrated north to work in the industrial cities of America. They also wanted to put bitter memories of the South behind them. But the stock market crash affected Michigan manufacturers no less than anyone else, and the streets of Detroit were crowded with men laid off from their jobs. Most were frustrated and angry. The fact that Whites often retained jobs while Blacks were among the first to go produced a potentially explosive situation.

W.D. Fard

Into this environment stepped a man who changed the course of American religious history. Very little is known about him, although guesses about his origin are many. Even his name is still a point of controversy: Farrad Mohammad, F. Mohammad Ali, Professor Ford, Wali Farrad and

W.D. Fard have all been suggested. The latter has been the most popular, and so it is the name we will use. Fard appeared on the streets of Detroit first as a peddler. He hawked items that he claimed were commonly used in the true homeland of Blacks across the sea. For people who at the time were leading essentially meaningless lives, stories of exotic foreign lands held great interest; they invited Fard to speak in many homes throughout the Black community.

His message was simple. The Black people of the United States had been deprived of their heritage by Whites, who had kidnaped and enslaved their ancestors during the three preceding centuries. They continued to oppress the Black race, albeit in a less direct manner. Rather than living in squalor, Blacks should be living in splendor—as Fard claimed that many of their foreign brothers and sisters were doing.

That many African-Americans had adopted Christianity—the religion of the slave masters—was nothing less than treason. The religion of Whites served no other purpose than to pacify and emasculate, focusing the attention of Blacks upon a future heaven rather than upon their current conditions. Such a distraction was, according to Fard, part of a conspiracy to keep Blacks in a subservient position.

Fard taught that the true religion of the Black man was Islam, a faith of dignity and empowerment. Blacks who desired to attain the status for which they were created must abandon the White beliefs and take up teachings and practices which were designed to liberate rather than subjugate.

Christianity was an outgrowth of Judaism—which in itself was highly problematic—and the Christian "reconstruction" of the life of the Prophet Jesus, as it appears in the Gospel accounts, glorified submission to the point of a humiliating execution as a common criminal.

A religion which glorified indignity, suffering and cruel death might well be a faith Blacks could identify with in their current situation. But such humiliating circumstances need not continue. Islam would guide African-Americans who sought the kind of life for which they had originally been destined.

In a relatively short time, Fard gathered enough followers to rent a hall he called a "Temple of Islam." This choice of terminology indicates to some that Fard or his early adherents had connections with the Moorish Science Temple of Noble Drew Ali, which was founded in 1913 as an eclectic mixture of Eastern thinking and classical Islam specifically designed for African-Americans.[1] Ali died in 1929, leaving a leadership vacuum that was not quickly filled. Several of the more discouraged joined themselves to Fard's new group.

From the beginning, Fard attempted to impart a sense of elitism to those who dedicated themselves to the movement. He authored *The Secret Ritual of the Nation of Islam*, which continues to be memorized by all devotees and is transmitted only orally. Another work, *Teaching for the Lost, Found Nation of Islam in a Mathematical Way*, appeared in written form but in a symbolic language; the interpretation was known only to Fard. For three years, the founder worked at developing a liturgy for the Temple worship services. He also founded an elementary and secondary school and a Muslim Girls Training Class to deal with the illiteracy that characterized much of the Black community.

Anticipating the same kind of opposition from Whites that Noble Drew Ali had experienced, he established a military wing called the Fruit of Islam to teach young men combat tactics, including the use of firearms. At this time, Fard appointed a Minister of Islam to assume leadership, and several assistant ministers were added to help administrate the rapidly growing organization.

Elijah Muhammad

Elijah Poole, a migrant from Georgia who had shown particular devotion to Fard, became the first Minister to be selected. Renamed Elijah Muhammad, he became Fard's right-hand man and heir-apparent of the movement, which by 1934 had attracted some 8,000 adherents. In June of that year Fard disappeared. Although it was hinted that this was a move by Elijah Muhammad to consolidate his own power, accusations of foul play were never proved, and Muhammad became Fard's successor. His original explanation was that Fard, having accomplished what he had come to America to do, had returned to the Middle East.

When a power struggle ensued, Muhammad moved from Detroit to Chicago's Temple No. 2, a move reminiscent of his namesake's migration from Mecca to Medina. Given breathing room, Elijah

Muhammad began to reshape the teachings into his own image. He elevated Fard and identified him with Allah; followers could thus worship and pray to him. From this it was only a short jump for Elijah Muhammad to equate himself with the original Muhammad, and he became known as the Prophet and Messenger of Allah.

His message was welcome to the African-American community of the 1930s. An emphasis on discipline and elitism provided meaning and purpose for men and women whose hope had reached a low ebb. Members of Muhammad's Nation of Islam were forbidden to drink alcohol, use tobacco, gamble, eat more than one meal per day or take out loans. It was expected that all members maintain steady employment even if their jobs were not high-paying. The movement strictly enforced standards of dress; neatness and cleanliness were paramount. A stable family life and faithfulness to one's spouse were considered essential.

According to C. Eric Lincoln, who was for decades the leading academic authority on African-American Islam, the greatest attraction of the Black Muslims had little to do with religion. Much more appealing was the idea of a group with enough solidarity and power to make a credible stand against the White race.[2]

Racial solidarity, then, was from the beginning the primary motivation behind African-American Islam. The movement became "the tie that binds" for many young Black males who had no sense of shared identity. The Nation of Islam thus became a "brotherhood," a forum for venting frustration at growing up Black in America and an environment in which one could experience sympathy and empathy from one's peers. The rapid growth of the movement and the fervor of its members imparted excitement and hope that something might actually be accomplished if enough of the Black race joined. Some social injustices might actually be addressed if the voices became loud and influential enough.

Redefining Allah

From the '40s through the early '70s, Elijah Muhammad continued to develop his organization's beliefs and practices. Gradually he formed doctrinal tenets and a subcultural worldview. He nuanced the original teaching that equated Fard with Allah. Fard became the fulfillment of a 6,000-year-old prophecy of Allah's incarnation on earth. But Allah became not a singular concept; indeed, all Blacks represent Allah, and it may even be said that African-Americans collectively *are* Allah.

Thus Allah is the Supreme Black Man, whereas the White man personifies the devil. The Caucasian race was created only 6,000 years ago by a Black scientist named Yakub who rebelled against Allah. In producing a hybrid race of humans without pigmentation, Yakub achieved the creation of a group of subhumans utterly lacking in humanity. The proof? Who but Whites have ever been guilty of such atrocities as the Holocaust, perpetrated by Whites against Whites? Christianity, disguised as a religion, is actually the master strategy of Whites for enslaving other peoples of the earth.

The Black man, on the other hand, has existed since the earth's creation. Thus African-Americans are the progenitors of the human race. With such a divine origin and noble calling, they must live as exemplary people. African-American Islam required prayers to be said at least five times per day. It forbade foods such as pork and corn bread—the former because of Muslim dietary laws, the latter because of its identification as a "slave food." Only a single meal was to be eaten each day, and Muslims who gained excess weight were fined.

Attendance at two Temple meetings per week was mandatory; failure to meet this requirement led to suspension and possibly expulsion from the Nation. Courtship or marriage outside the group was discouraged, and the conduct of spouses was expected to be above reproach. Fornication and adultery were condemned. These and other regulations produced a number of exemplary persons who became role models for outsiders.

Perhaps the most controversial aspect of the movement was its insistence upon an absolute separation of the Black and White races. From the beginning, Elijah Muhammad demanded a section of the United States which would become a true "Nation of Islam" territorially and politically. At first he demanded two or three states, then four or five. By 1960, no less than nine or ten states would be sufficient.

But such grandiose schemes were never realized, and during the 1960s, the movement began to falter. The American Black community did not support the views of Elijah Muhammad, which frustrated the leader and his followers. Most African-Americans remained Christian in some sense of the word. Rather than calling for separation between the races, they devoted their energies to reconciliation and cooperation.

Muhammad could never cooperate with "the devil," but only a minority of American Blacks favored such an extremist view. Black intellectuals virtually ignored the Nation of Islam, and organizations such as the NAACP had their own agendas—which did not include the goals of Muhammad. Black leader Thurgood Marshall believed that Black Muslims were nothing more than criminals with financial backing from foreign powers.

Such pronouncements from the Black community influenced the United States government's view of the Nation. The FBI employed agents to keep an eye on the activities and movements of the major personalities within Muhammad's organization. Attempts by the Japanese to gain control of the group prior to World War II put a stigma on the movement from the very beginning, and during the Cold War era it became a simple matter to connect the organization with communist insurgency. A number of Congressmen during the 1950s considered Muhammad a Soviet agent bent on overthrowing the U.S. government and undermining American civil liberties.

Even more significant was the criticism received from the ethnic Muslim community and world Islam. From its inception, the Nation of Islam was considered by all ethnic Muslims to be a heretical sect rather than a new indigenous expression of the

Muslim faith. It is not difficult to understand this attitude. Like others, Muslims saw that Elijah Muhammad was not committed to Islamic orthodoxy or to spreading the faith among African-Americans, but to the social plight of Black people. He was using Islam to provide a unifying ideology for Blacks.

In order to accomplish this, he created a pseudo-theology bearing almost no relation to orthodox Islam. The idea that Allah had incarnated himself in W.D. Fard and that Elijah Muhammad was a new "Prophet" equal to the original Muhammad was heresy enough. Theology concerning the origin of the Black and White races and the justification of racial separation only increased the distance between the two forms of Islam.

If the criticisms of ethnic Muslims had remained external to Muhammad's movement, there would have been little effect. But the transformation in the life of one of Elijah Muhammad's most trusted lieutenants changed the course of the movement forever.

Malcolm X

The man known as Minister Malcolm X Shabazz was born Malcolm Little. His conversion to the Black Muslim movement came in 1947 while he was serving time for robbery at a maximum security facility in Concord, Massachusetts. Upon his release in 1952, Malcolm became completely devoted to the cause of the Nation of Islam and a personal favorite of Elijah Muhammad. Besides assuming the prestigious position of Minister of Temple No.

7 in Harlem, he was appointed National Minister early in 1963. Until the end of that year, only brotherhood and respect apparently existed between the two men.

But then an inflammatory remark made by Malcolm concerning the assassination of President John Kennedy led to his ninety-day suspension from the movement. Some believe that this incident was an excuse to bring into the open a rift that already existed behind the scenes. Indeed, documentation exists that the FBI exploited this division in order to split the movement and isolate the charismatic Malcolm.[3]

Rather than returning to the Nation of Islam after his suspension, Malcolm withdrew entirely and founded The Muslim Mosque, Incorporated. One arm of this agency was the Organization of Afro-American Unity, which was perhaps better known than the parent group. During 1964 Malcolm spent a great deal of time traveling in Africa and the Middle East. In the midst of these journeys, he performed the pilgrimage to Mecca and learned for the first time the vast differences between the teachings of Elijah Muhammad and those of orthodox Islam. After returning to the United States, he highlighted these differences and denounced the movement in which he had formerly played such an important part.

This teaching led to chaos in the Black community and, allegedly, to Malcolm's assassination in February of 1965. As so often happens, Malcolm's death increased his significance and influence. Many perceived him as a martyr for the cause of true Islam. Suspicions naturally fell upon Elijah Muhammad and his followers, raising concerns regarding the Nation of Islam.[4]

In the 1970s, Americans had the war in Vietnam and the beginnings of the Watergate scandal on their minds. With enactment of the Civil Rights Acts around the country, and with African-American soldiers dying beside White Americans in the jungles of Southeast Asia, Elijah Muhammad's rhetoric began to take on a faded tenor.

With concerns about pollution, gas shortages and inflation, Americans realized that the materialistic "rush" of the 1950s might be gone forever. America's Blacks—like nearly everyone else—prepared for an increasingly bleak future. In this context, Elijah Muhammad's announcement in 1972 that he planned to build a $500,000 mansion for himself in Chicago—as well as four other mansions for family members—brought a storm of controversy. Some denounced such a grandiose plan, while others defended it as the prerogative of a "Prophet of God" who deserved even more.

As age began to overtake the Nation of Islam's leader, speculation arose regarding his successor. Would his son-in-law Raymond Sharrieff succeed him, or one of his six sons? Predictions were rife that a tremendous power struggle would follow Muhammad's death.

On February 25, 1975, Muhammad succumbed to congestive heart failure. The next day his son Wallace D. was designated successor. Did Muhammad have any inkling of how his son would change the organization he had labored so long to develop?

For many it is a complete mystery as to why Wallace, who had been suspended and even excommunicated from the movement a number of times, was chosen to take the reins. We will look into the transforming work of Wallace D. in the next chapter.

Louis Farrakhan

Wallace D.'s radical revamping of the movement was not a happy change for all African-American Muslims. Consequently, several offshoots claimed to be the spiritual continuation of Elijah Muhammad's Nation of Islam. But only one leader was able to achieve the stature of Elijah Muhammad: Louis Walcott (or Wilcott), better known as Louis Farrakhan.

At the time of Malcolm X's assassination, Farrakhan was minister of the Boston Temple. A vocalist and musician, his entertainment skills made him a popular figure. Leaders designated him Malcolm's successor and gave him the task of reconstructing the Harlem Temple. He was eminently successful in this assignment until Elijah Muhammad's death.

Many had anticipated that Farrakhan would succeed the founder, and Wallace's appointment was not well received in New York. Farrakhan pledged his support to Wallace, however, and this ended the controversy until the Nation of Islam began taking a new direction. Farrakhan believed that Elijah Muhammad had never intended for the Nation to become an orthodox Islamic denomination, and in

November 1977 he announced his intention to return the movement to its original form.

The beginning of Farrakhan's group was not auspicious. While estimates of African-American Islam are notoriously unreliable, it has been suggested that only about 20,000 of the approximately 2 million Black Muslims living in America at that time joined his movement. Some twenty years later, the proportions were essentially the same, although there is still dispute regarding exact figures. One report in 1994 indicated that there were between 70,000 and 100,000,[5] while *Newsweek* reported in 1995 that the Nation had only about 20,000 members—the same number as when Farrakhan began in 1977.[6]

In any case, out of a total population of some 2.6 million African-American Muslims, no more than three percent belong to Farrakhan's movement. The overwhelming majority belong to the organization of Wallace D. Muhammad. The ethnic Muslim communities consider Wallace D.'s followers members of orthodox Islam. They no longer call themselves "Black Muslims" but simply "Muslims."

Despite its minority status, Farrakhan's group receives nearly all the media attention given to African-American Islam. This is more a commentary on the American media (which seems to prefer extreme and even hysterical events) than it is upon the two groups. Farrakhan's anti-White and anti-Jewish rhetoric receives instant press and keeps racism on both sides raw and inflamed.

Even the demand for a complete separation of the races still enjoys currency. I have seen a redrawn map of the United States that shows a line following the Continental Divide through the Rocky Mountains. Land to the west of the line is to be reserved for Caucasian Americans, Hispanics and others, with the capital being Hayden Lake, Idaho—renowned for its connection with White supremacist groups. All territory to the east would become the Nation of Islam with Chicago as its New Jerusalem. The five boroughs of New York City would be walled off and become a modern ghetto for Jewish people called Hymietown.[7]

While this kind of hate-mongering and divisiveness appears in newspapers and magazines across the country, Wallace Muhammad's organization—now known as the Ministry of Warith Deen Muhammad after Wallace's name change—works behind the scenes with African-American prison inmates and inner-city development programs. So significant are Wallace's changes that, far from arousing government suspicion, his organization signed a contract in 1979 with the U.S. Department of Defense to provide a new version of C-rations for the military.[8]

Splinter Groups

These two movements include the vast majority of African-American Muslims, but several smaller organizations may be encountered in the cities of America, particularly New York, Chicago and Los Angeles.

The Nation of Gods and Earths

An organization called the Five Percenters, for instance, separated from Elijah Muhammad's Nation of Islam in 1964. Also known as The Nation of Gods and Earths, their founder was Clarence "Pudding" 13X. He taught that his followers comprised the chosen five percent of humanity who live a righteous "Islamic" life and thus manifest the "true divine nature of the Black man who is God or Allah."[9]

In this group, eighty-five percent of the world's population are considered to be uncivilized and completely ignorant of God. Ten percent teach lies to the poor people of the world, such as the idea that the Living God is a "spook" (spirit). Included in this number are orthodox Muslims who are "bloodsuckers" of the poor. The remaining five percent of mankind is the special elite of God; indeed, they *are* God.

Espousing many of Elijah Muhammad's beliefs regarding the origin and nature of the Black race vis-a-vis the Whites, the Five Percenters have turned to electronic media to disseminate their beliefs and practices. They dominate the rap music industry through artists such as Rakim, Big Daddy Kane and Lakim Shabazz, who write Black Muslim theology into their lyrics. They also use radio talk shows to spread their teaching.[10]

Although Clarence 13X was assassinated in June of 1969, his followers have carried on and adapted well to the tremendous cultural changes in American society since the early 1960s. Members of the group are powerfully eloquent and make full use of African-American street slang, which many young Blacks find highly appealing.

Like Farrakhan's Nation of Islam, this group's agenda is racially motivated. They teach that Blacks are the "original people of earth," that they are the "mothers and fathers of civilization," that they should be educated so as to become self-sufficient as a people, that Blacks are God (using his proper name Allah, which stands for Arm Leg Leg Arm Head), and that the unified "Black Family" is any nation's most important building block.[11]

Innovative teachings also include a subordinate role for women; indeed, the new name of the group (The Nation of Gods and Earths) derives from the teaching that men are to be seen as gods while women have the status of earths, also known as "queens." "Earths" cover their hair and wear long dresses, while "gods" commonly wear *kufis* (Muslim skull caps). The group consists mainly of young persons who, as they grow older, often seek the security of orthodox Sunni Islam.

Ansarullah Nubian Islamic Hebrews

Another group commonly seen on the street corners of New York City is the Ansarullah Nubian Islamic Hebrews, a group founded by Dwight York in the mid-1960s. After his conversion, York changed his name to Isa Abdullah and began to preach a concoction of Islam and Black nationalism to New York City African-American youth. He gathered followers into a group which in 1967 he named the Ansar Pure Sufi; his symbol became the star of David inside a crescent with an *ankh* (an ancient Egyptian symbol) inside the star. In 1969 the group's name became Nubian Islamic Hebrews, and a crescent and spear were added to the group's symbol.

During the 1970s and 1980s Isa embellished his claims. He first said he was the *mujaddid*, or renewer of the Islamic religion, for the current Islamic century. Then he claimed to be the Messiah whose second coming is predicted in Islamic eschatology. In 1985, he proclaimed himself the incarnation of Allah for this age.

As with the Five Percenters, the Ansarullah have made productive use of music, giving several rhythm-and-blues, rap and pop musicians their start to fame. The Ansar live communally to duplicate the original Muslim community of the Prophet and to remain separated from "unbelievers." This term "unbelievers" is used broadly; indeed, it includes not only Jews and Europeans, but also a number of orthodox Muslims, especially the Saudi Arabians, who are accused of "Arab sectism."

Some of the more interesting deviations of the Ansarullah's teachings from orthodox Islamic doctrine include the following beliefs:

- A pantheistic view of Allah—He is to be identified with all that is.

- Whites are not human—they have neither soul nor spirit. In addition, Black women have no spirit, only a soul.

- Ninety-nine percent of the *hadith* (traditions) are unreliable.

- The Bible is equal to the Qur'an, but lay persons should avoid the many false and distorted translations of both. (Isa, however, never says what *should* be read. In addition, Isa alone has access to other scriptures.)

- All of the prophets of Allah were Black; Adam was created from "the rich black soil of the Sudan."

- Jesus was the son of the archangel Gabriel, who cohabited with Mary to produce a being who was half-man, half-angel.

- All will enter hell for a time; it is not eternal, but rather a place of punishment and purification.

- Worship of Allah is to be mainly on the Sabbath, the seventh day of the week.

- The *hajj* is, in effect, denied to most followers due to the poverty and isolation forced upon them by the group.

- It is not only permissible but actually advisable to drink alcoholic beverages and to engage in oral and anal sexual intercourse.

- In the community, men must wear the Sudanese *jalabiya* and the women must cover their entire persons, exposing only their eyes.[12]

This group obviously deviates from orthodox Islam and the teachings of the Nation of Islam in a variety of ways. It has evolved through the years and continues in a state of flux even today. In the early 1990s Isa changed his name to Rabbani Y'shua Bar El Haady and now calls his group "The Saviors." He moved headquarters from New York to Atlanta and no longer addresses God as "Allah" but as Yahuwa Eloh.[13]

Other Groups

In addition to the Five Percenters and the Saviors, other communities include the Moorish Science Temple of America, the Islamic Party of North America, the Darul Islam, the United Nation of Islam, Minister John Muhammad's Nation of Islam, Imam Jamil Al-Amin's Darul Islam and two Sufi communities—the Naqshabandiyyah and the Tijaniyyah, whose members are primarily of African-American descent. All of these organizations are limited in membership and primarily localized. A brief description of each (with the exception of the United Nation of Islam) appears in Aminah McCloud's book, *African American Islam*.[14]

The information above could easily give the reader the impression that Islam—or more accurately, a deviant form of the religion—is making deep inroads into the African-American community. This may well trouble evangelicals, for traditionally they have seen Blacks as upholding a conservative form of the Christian faith. Thus some observers have concluded that a significant shift is underway in American society, one that could lead to Islam as the dominant religion in Black urban areas by 2020.[15] While many disagree, all ministers of the gospel—be they Black or White—are keeping a close eye on African-American Islam.

How Will the Church Respond?

The chief complaints against Christianity are apparently that the Church is too irrelevant to everyday "street life" and too oriented toward women. The movements of Farrakhan and Warith Deen Muhammad, on the other hand, are known for rehabilitating drug addicts, enforcing conservative dress codes which protect Black women, and promoting and modeling strong family structures to turn around the chaos existing within the Black community.

It is undeniable, however, that much of the appeal of African-American Islam comes because many Blacks feel that Christians have not taken a sufficiently proactive approach to eliminating racial tensions. Race relations have recently become increasingly important in Christian circles. This topic was the national theme of the Promise Keepers' events, for instance. This may slow the attrition rate from Christianity somewhat, but it is too soon to tell if the emphasis will have a lasting effect.

More insidious than the actual defections from Black churches is the dilution of Christian doctrine brought about by Louis Farrakhan's recent overtures to African-American congregations. *Christianity Today* reported in 1994 that Farrakhan has been quietly building contacts within churches and recently invited some 2,000 Christian leaders to dinner at his home in Chicago to discuss joint projects.[16] Much would depend upon what kind of cooperation these African-American Christians have in mind. But danger comes when the distinctions between Islam and Christianity are downplayed or completely submerged in favor of a sociological focus such as racial unity. History teaches that the gospel message will likely take a backseat to humanistic, political interests.

With regard to gender issues, some men and women may indeed be lured by the exotic—and manly—face of Islam. Young Black men are certainly finding a sense of fulfillment in a male-oriented faith. But will Black women in general wear head coverings and submit to their husbands? African-American women have a long tradition of independence. It hearkens back to the days of slavery, when marriages were nonexistent and men and women were bred on many Southern plantations like cattle.

This independence continued after emancipation within African-American churches. Even congregations with male pastors, elders and deacons were often under heavy behind-the-scenes influence by matriarchs. It is highly unlikely that most women will voluntarily abandon this structure. Indeed, some writers predict that in the future we may see a situation in which Black women will go to churches while the men go to the mosques.[17]

One may also question whether more radical steps of some churches to contextualize their theology and praxis for a Black audience will slow defections of young Blacks to Islam. Will ministers wearing *kente* cloth, African drums during worship services, depictions of the Hebrew patriarchs (along with Jesus, Mary and the disciples) as Blacks or the proclamation of Jesus as a revolutionary liberating the oppressed produce African-American churches that contain biblical truth? Or will African-American young people in these churches merely receive Black nationalism wrapped in a sub-biblical theological cloak? These are questions the African-American community, along with its White brothers and sisters, need to address.

Notes

1   For more information on this movement, see Yvonne Yazbeck Haddad and Jane Idleman Smith, *Mission to America: Five Islamic Sectarian Communities in North America* (Gainesville, FL: University Press of Florida, 1993).
2   See C. Eric Lincoln, *The Black Muslims in America*, 3rd ed. (Grand Rapids, MI: Eerdmans/ Trenton, NJ: Africa World Press, 1994), 26.
3   See Mattias Gardell, "The Sun of Islam Will Rise in the West: Minister Farrakhan and the Nation of Islam in the Latter Days," in *Muslim Communities in North America*, ed. Yvonne Yazbeck Haddad and Jane Idleman Smith (Albany, NY: State University of New York Press, 1994).
4   Three men were convicted and sentenced to life in prison for the murder of Malcolm X. Two of these had definite connections to Elijah Muhammad's Nation of Islam, though Muhammad adamantly disclaimed direct involvement in the assassination.
5   Gardell, 269.
6   Carla Power and Allison Samuels, "Battling for Souls," *Newsweek*, 30 October 1995, 47.
7   See, for instance, James McKeever, "Forecast for 1986-1987," *End-Times News Digest*, January 1986, 3.
8   C. Eric Lincoln, "The American Muslim Mission in the Context of American Social History," in *The Muslim Community in North America*, ed. Earle H. Waugh, Baha Abu-Laban and Regula B. Qureshi (Edmonton, Alberta: University of Alberta Press, 1983), 229.
9   See Yusuf Nuruddin, "The Five Percenters: A Teenage Nation of Gods and Earths," in *Muslim Communities*, ed. Yvonne Yazbeck Haddad and Jane Idleman Smith, 109.
10 Ibid., 112.
11 Cited in Ibid., 113.
12 See Abu Ameenah Bilal Phillips, *The Ansar Cult in America* (Riyadh, Saudi Arabia: Tawheed Publications, 1988), 20-119 passim.

13 In addition to the work of Phillips cited above, see Haddad and Smith, *Mission to America*, chapter 5.
14 See Aminah McCloud, *African American Islam* (Los Angeles: Routledge, 1995).
15 See Andres Tapia, "Churches Wary of Inner-city Islamic Inroads," *Christianity Today*, 10 January 1994, 36.
16 Ibid., 38.
17 Power and Samuels, "Battling for Souls," 46.

6

The Ministry of
W. Deen Muhammad

When Elijah Muhammad died on February 25, 1975, leadership of the African-American Nation of Islam fell to his son, Wallace D. Muhammad. From the moment he took office, Wallace made it clear that his goal was full integration of the Nation into world Islam. One must assume that to be designated as Elijah Muhammad's successor, he must have hidden his designs from his father or convinced him of the benefits of orthodox Islam. C. Eric Lincoln intimates that implementation of this "grand vision" had been a goal since the days of Wallace's temple leadership in Philadelphia in the 1950s.[1]

Not surprisingly, the sudden transition of the group into a new paradigm met with disappointment. A number of members of the Nation felt betrayed, and when Louis Farrakhan stepped forward in 1977 to revive Elijah Muhammad's original vision, he drew an immediate following. From the media coverage that Farrakhan receives today, it is easy to understand how the American public might believe that his followers comprise a majority of African-American Muslims. This has never been the case, however. Most observers believe that Farrakhan was able to attract no more than 20,000 persons, while well over a million Blacks remained loyal to Wallace.

Moving Away from Racism

A variety of reasons account for a large majority remaining under the designated heir's leadership. Wallace was the founder's son, and some of his famous father's charisma was assumed to have passed to him. In addition, a large number of African-Americans had apparently tired of the Black nationalist rhetoric, the upraised fists of defiance and the constant controversy which surrounded the movement. The antiestablishment and anti-White orientation of the original Nation of Islam had indeed united Blacks under a single banner, but it had also marginalized and isolated African-Americans even more. Acceptance into the global community of the world's 1 billion Muslims was for many a welcome prospect.

Wallace immediately distanced his movement from the former Nation of Islam. Many leaders were demoted or reassigned, the organization's paramilitary wing was disbanded and a new financial structure implemented. He reinterpreted or abandoned many of Elijah Muhammad's more far-fetched teachings, such as the Black scientist Yakub and the origin of the Black and White races.

Perhaps the most significant changes involved the attitude of Black Muslims toward Whites. Under Elijah Muhammad, epithets such as "blue-eyed archenemies" and "White devils" had been common. In the title "Black Muslim," stress had been laid at least as much on "Black" as on the idea of "Muslim." But Wallace denounced this polarization, insisting that Whites be allowed to become full members of any of the *masjids* under his jurisdiction. He also disavowed "Black Muslims," the appellation of members of his organization.

Embracing America

A transformation occurred, as well, in the attitude of the group toward the United States. During the reign of Elijah Muhammad, the organization looked upon the U.S. as a White bastion, an aggressive and repressive nation built upon the backs of the Africans who had been brought forcibly to America and enslaved. Wallace himself still speaks of the influence that this environment once had upon him but now claims to be an American patriot and firm believer in the Constitution.[2]

Wallace now believes that both Blacks and Whites have made progress. All schools under the auspices of his organization display an American flag and students recite the Pledge of Allegiance along with morning prayers. But much to his surprise, Wallace found that American people in general were unprepared or unreceptive to African-Americans entering mainstream American society. Instead of warmhearted approval, his actions and statements have since the beginning met with suspicion.[3]

Becoming Global Muslims

While the title "Black Muslim" fell rapidly into disrepute, it seemed inappropriate for African-Americans to be called simply "Muslims." So the term "Bilalians" was coined in honor of Bilal ibn Rabah, one of the original companions of the Prophet Muhammad. The official newspaper of the organization, *Muhammad Speaks*, became *The Bilalian News*.

Other changes, however, reflected the new leader's desire to integrate his people with the Muslim world at large. The fast of Ramadan had been celebrated under Elijah Muhammad during the month of December. Now Wallace scheduled it to coincide with the period determined by the lunar calendar of the global community of Islam. He allowed women to take on new roles, permitted men to enlist in the armed forces of the United States and encouraged participation in the American political process. The heretofore tarnished reputation of Malcolm X was refurbished and the Harlem *masjid* was renamed in his honor.

In 1976 the organization's name was changed to The World Community of Al-Islam in the West, a somewhat clumsy title but one which indicated the movement's new direction. By 1981, however, the name's cumbersomeness dictated yet another change. The group became known as The American Muslim Mission, a shorter title which communicated dynamism and purpose.

During these years Wallace began introducing himself as Warith Deen Muhammad rather than the former "Wallace D." He explained that there were too many "symbolic and mystical" meanings connected with the name Wallace. He was referring to the "unIslamic teachings" of Elijah Muhammad's mentor Wallace Fard, after whom he had been named.

One goal carried over from the original Nation of Islam was elevating as many African-Americans as possible socially and economically. Prior to Wallace's leadership, such endeavors were limited to cottage industries and to linking the unemployed to the comparatively few African-Americans with their own businesses. This system had worked fairly well, but Wallace wanted to expand possibilities for employment.

The turn of the organization to a more "pro-America" stance brought about an unexpected dividend. In 1979 the World Community of Al-Islam in the West received a contract from the U.S. Department of Defense valued at some $22 million. Members of Wallace's organization were to team up with Allen Cheng and Associates to manufacture a new and improved version of C-rations for use by the U.S. armed forces. At the time it was estimated that proper marketing of these materials would yield at least $60 million per year. This was a great boon for the organization from the standpoint of finances and the credibility gained from its connections with the United States government.

Earning Public Trust

Gradually the reorganized movement, along with its leader, began to earn the public trust. By 1983 Wallace had received the Walter Reuther Humanities Award and the Four Freedoms Award (an honor shared by such persons as John F. Kennedy and Eleanor Roosevelt). Acceptance was also growing within the global Islamic community. In 1978 the nations of Saudi Arabia, Abu Dhabi and Qatar named Wallace the sole trustee for the distribution of funds to all Muslim organizations engaged in the propagation of faith in the United States.[4] Wallace was also the only American observer to be invited to the Tenth Annual Islamic Conference of Ministers of Foreign Affairs, held in Fez, Morocco, in the early 1980s.

The attention these invitations and honors garnered was not altogether welcome to Wallace. Accusations began to appear in print regarding an alleged "manipulation" of his organization by "foreign powers." Perhaps to allay such suspicions, Wallace took deliberate steps in 1985 to decentralize his following and to dismantle its political orientations. Since that time the organization—known today simply as The Ministry of W. Deen Muhammad—has for the most part emphasized the purely *religious* aspects of Islam rather than its social and political applications.

This is not to say that Wallace and his followers ignore social and political issues. But they cast these comments very differently than Elijah Muhammad and Louis Farrakhan. A speech delivered to the Los Angeles World Affairs Council in 1993 illustrates this. Rather than heaping execration upon the Jews as Farrakhan has been continually accused of doing, Wallace emphasized the common roots of Jews, Christians and Muslims.

The adherents of Islam, Wallace has said, are a people whom God created for the purpose of serving all peoples. Muslims do not seek worldly dominance, despite what the historical *jihads* may appear to indicate. Islam promotes the rights of all, including women. The only reason that Islam does not appear to uphold women's rights is because Western colonialism warped the view that Muslims had of their own faith. While this sentiment could easily be construed as indicating that some bitterness remains regarding the past, Wallace makes it clear that since colonialism has now (at least for the most part) faded away, a time for healing has been introduced which will bring Muslims back to the principles and practices of true Islam.

Wielding Quiet Influence

Today Wallace lives in Little Rock, Arkansas, from where he flies every Tuesday to the Chicago area. Having long ago sold the palatial mansion of his father to Louis Farrakhan, he operates out of a small office in the basement of his daughter's home in Calumet City, a suburb just south of Chicago.

While in the city he tapes his weekly television broadcast about the Muslim world and Islamic culture and oversees the production of his organization's weekly newspaper, *The Muslim Journal*.

His ministry currently claims to oversee some 1.5 million believers, but there are only about 100 formally organized mosques, or *masjids*. Responsibility for these is spread among twenty-three *imams* who are loosely connected with each other.[5] Donations received by Wallace himself total no more than $7,000 to $10,000 per month.[6]

Recently Wallace has been spending more time in the New York City area. In 1994 he purchased twelve acres of land where he plans to build a third home for his family. He will use this as a base to gain contacts among the estimated 1 million Muslims living in New York and New Jersey. His goal, however, is not to control or manipulate these individuals; therefore, his leadership style differs greatly from Farrakhan's. The *New York Times* reports that Wallace "usually travels alone, carrying his own bag. He does not have or want, he says, any direct control over his followers."[7]

Because he does not want to maintain a specific geographic or denominational territory, he is free to travel and speak on behalf of Islam and Muslims of the world in a variety of contexts. A sample listing of his activities in the past ten years includes:

- In 1988 he participated as a Muslim representative at the World Parliament of Religious Leaders Meeting for "Survival of the Earth and Its Environment" in Oxford, England.

- Also in 1988 he participated in the symbolic signing of the First Amendment Charter for Religious Freedom in Williamsburg, Virginia, as the representative for the Muslims of America.

- In 1990 he led a delegation of Muslim leaders, scholars and educators to Saudi Arabia where he addressed the Islamic Conference on the Persian Gulf conflict, also as the representative for the Muslims of America.

- In 1992 he delivered an address at the Pentagon on the fundamentals of Islam to chaplains in the U.S. military.

- In 1992 he became the first Muslim leader to deliver an invocation on the floor of the U.S. Senate and to address the Georgia State Legislature.

- In 1993, he represented Islam at the Inaugural Interfaith Prayer service hosted by President Bill Clinton.

- On December 7, 1993, he addressed the Los Angeles World Affairs Council on the topic "Islam and Universal Values: How Muslims Are to Contribute to World Peace."

- In October 1994 the Mufti Abdullah Mukhtar, representing the former Soviet Union's 60 million Muslims, met with Wallace as the representative of Muslims of America at the Masjid Bilal in Cleveland, Ohio.

- In December 1994, Wallace was awarded the "Cup of Compassion" Award by Hartford Seminary for his work in improving Muslim, Christian and Jewish relations.

- In 1995 Wallace was selected as the International President for the World Conference on Religion and Peace; he addressed the Governing Board in Copenhagen, Denmark.

- On March 26, 1995, Wallace delivered the keynote address at a Muslim-Jewish Convocation billed as "the first serious public dialogue between the top leaders of Islam and Reform Judaism."

- In May of 1995, *Forbes* magazine invited Wallace to its Forbes Forum Conference to address the participants on the topic "How Do We Save Our Youth?"

- In December of 1995 Wallace visited Saudi Arabia at the invitation of King Fahd to participate in discussions on how to improve the curriculum of Muslim schools in America.

We find that Warith Deen Muhammad has acquired international stature while maintaining humility and a service orientation. He is reported to be greatly troubled by the media attention lavished on Louis Farrakhan, who, he believes, gives the wrong impression of Islam. Farrakhan's fiery rhetoric wins him headlines and television spots, while Wallace is quiet and retiring and spends as much time as possible with his family. (He has been married three times and has eight children.)

Some might feel that he could do much more for Islam if he adopted a more powerful style. But the activities and achievements noted above demonstrate that his quieter approach has earned him a credibility within the global Islamic community that Farrakhan and others like him will never attain.

For this reason, we evangelical Christians must consider Warith Deen Muhammad a more formidable competitor for the souls of men and women than Louis Farrakhan. The quiet influence of Elijah Muhammad's heir upon his 1.5 million followers will likely be of more lasting significance than the emotional frenzy produced by the current leader of the Nation of Islam.

Notes

1 C. Eric Lincoln, "The American Muslim Mission in the Context of American Social History," in *The Muslim Community in North America*, ed. Earle H. Waugh, Baha Abu-Laban and Regula B. Qureshi (Edmonton, Alberta: University of Alberta Press, 1983), 228.
2 Cited in ibid., 230.
3 From an interview with Dirk Sager, correspondent for ZDF, German television; "Communicating for Survival," World Community of Islam [WSI] news release, 27 December 1979; cited in Lincoln, "American Muslim Mission," 227-228.
4 Lincoln, "American Muslim Mission," 230-231.
5 See "In the Muslim Mainstream," *The Christian Century*, 26 October 1994, 978-979.
6 Steven Barboza, *American Jihad: Islam after Malcolm X* (New York: Doubleday, 1994), 97.
7 Don Terry, "Black Muslims Enter Islamic Mainstream," *New York Times*, Monday, 3 May 1993, B7.

7

Louis Farrakhan and the Nation of Islam Today

Carl F. Ellis, Jr.

Among African-Americans, Islam has been growing at an explosive rate. Currently about 2.6 million African-American Muslims live in the United States, divided among at least seventeen major sects ranging from nonracial orthodox to radical Black separatist. While many have been puzzled by the seemingly sudden rise of Islam, the social and theological forces behind this upsurge have been brewing for about 100 years.

Today, many issues close to the hearts of African-Americans largely remain unaddressed by the church—both the traditional African-American church and the White church, including "evangelicals" and "liberals." On the other hand, many young African-Americans perceive the Islamic community as addressing their issues. Therefore, the lion's share of those who are seeking God continue to move toward the mosque. This is ironic because the Bible more adequately addresses African-American concerns than does the Qur'an. Today's Islamic growth in the United States owes more to the weakness and retreat of the church than it does to the strength and veracity of Islam. Let's look at how and why this situation developed.

Theological Vacuum

Though Louis Farrakhan leads less than one percent (18,000-20,000) of African-American Muslims, his influence in popular Black culture far exceeds the limits of the Nation of Islam he leads. In fact, if asked, "What name comes to mind when you think of Islam in North America?" a significant cross section of Americans would answer, "Louis Farrakhan." Even among many churchgoing African-Americans, his influence is considerable. Church leaders who lament Farrakhan's growing influence often try to counteract it through greater effort. But too often these well-meaning Christian brothers and sisters do not realize that their message is inadequate—not the biblical message itself, but the theology they espouse.

Like all Bible-believing communities, the historic African-American church preached Christ crucified and risen and the doctrine of salvation by grace through faith. Like the struggle for freedom and dignity, historic African-American theology developed along two streams: Northern and Southern. In both cases, an overarching theological theme and biblical paradigm developed for doing ministry. The resulting ministry models worked out and applied the church's faith to the surrounding community.

In the antebellum South where slavery was king, there developed a theology of *suffering*. The paradigm which emerged was "the Exodus." The slaves identified with the children of Israel in Egyptian bondage and saw the hand of God at work in their hope for deliverance. This theology addressed issues such as survival, refuge and resistance to oppression.

In the antebellum North where slavery had died out, a theology of *empowerment* began to develop. The paradigm became "the Exile." The freedmen sensed a special calling from God to bring the gospel of Christ to the rest of the African diaspora (people of African descent living in the South, Canada, the Caribbean, South America and Africa) and beyond. Had it fully developed, this theology would have addressed issues such as dignity, identity and the divine significance of the African-American experience.

With the official end of slavery in 1865,[1] the former slaves were devastated and confused about who they were and why they were here.

Yet the Post Civil War Reconstruction set the stage for astounding economic, political and social progress by African-Americans. The need for the theology of suffering was declining. The exodus paradigm was being realized. Therefore, the

Southern church adopted the Northern church's developing theology of empowerment. By 1870, the indigenous African-American church was experiencing explosive growth because the above-mentioned core cultural issues were being addressed theologically.

The paradigm of the exile which developed in the North during the late eighteenth and early nineteenth centuries was the beginning of the "Pan-African" vision. Under this banner, the African-American church became actively involved in cultural and economic development here in the U.S. and in missions overseas, especially in Africa.

This period also saw the development of the "Afrocentric" vision. This is why so many early African-American churches and Christian organizations had "African" in their names. These included the *African* Baptist Churches, the *African* Methodist Episcopal Churches (AME), AME Zion Churches, the Free *African* Society and the *African* Presbyterian Churches, to name a few. These early African-American Christians were committed to Christ, yet they were clearly identified with Africa. Why?

Unlike the terms "colored" and "Negro," "African" was not a label of inferiority imposed upon them by the dominant culture. Thus, "African" became the term of choice, leaving room for true humanity (being in God's image) and their emerging ethnic identity. Citing Romans 12:2— "Do not conform any longer to the pattern of this world, but be transformed by the renewing of your mind. Then you will be able to test and approve what God's will is—his good, pleasing and perfect will"—they found the balance between their ethnicity as Africans and their universality as Christians.

However, three events between 1875 and 1900 radically altered the theological direction of the African-American church.

- First, with 1877 came the end of Post Civil War Reconstruction in the South. The 1876 presidential election pitted Rutherford B. Hayes (a Republican) against Samuel J. Tilden (a Democrat). The tally of the electoral college was so close that both candidates declared victory. A congressional commission had to settle the dispute. The Democrats agreed to concede the election to Hayes on the condition that Hayes would agree to withdraw federal troops from the Democrats' stronghold in the South.[2] These troops had been protecting slaves from increasing White hostility and enforcing the provisions of the Thirteenth, Fourteenth and Fifteenth Amendments.[3]

    By April 20, 1877, the federal troops were gone and Reconstruction was over. The former slaves were thereby abandoned to the devices of those who wanted to establish a system of neoslavery. Within a decade, the remarkable progress of Blacks in the South was nullified. By then, White supremacy was firmly reestablished in the South through terrorism (the Ku Klux Klan), political disenfranchisement (through the "poll tax" and bogus "literacy tests"), racial segregation laws (the "Black codes") and exploitive economic relationships (e.g., the sharecropper system).[4]

- Secondly, with the industrial revolution in the North came a massive wave of European immigration. This led to the rise of White-only trade unions. The result was the elimination of African-Americans from the skilled labor force within one generation.

  Accompanying the industrial revolution was the development of the "melting pot" concept. All immigrants to America were pressured to forsake their cultural roots and assimilate into the "American" way of life, consisting largely of British and northern European (Protestant) cultural values. The more one's indigenous culture contained these values, the greater was one's ability to "melt." Those from other parts of the world who tried to "melt" found it difficult or impossible. The result of this was the exclusion of African-Americans from mainstream American life and the development of institutional racism.

- Thirdly, the Congress of Berlin (1878) and the Conference of Berlin (1884-1885) resulted in the consolidation of European colonialism in Africa. No Africans were present at these meetings. The colonial authorities then began a systematic program of barring entry to new African-American missionaries and expelling those already there. As a result, the missions activity of the African-American church was decimated.

These "three great traumas" had significant effects on the African-American church. Not only was the church caught off guard by these traumas, but concern for survival became the overwhelming issue. The missions consciousness of the church was obliterated. The developing theology of empowerment was abandoned. The church reverted to the theology of suffering which had developed during slavery. Thus, a theological vacuum developed in terms of empowerment and its related issues. By 1910, the explosive growth of the church had ended.

Several non-Christian and quasi-Christian efforts attempted to fill this vacuum. Among them were 1) W.E.B. Du Bois' advocacy of solidarity through education; 2) a few Black Jewish sects; 3) Marcus Garvey and the United Negro Improvement Association (U.N.I.A.) and 4) several Black nationalist Islamic sects.

Noble Drew Ali

The first of these Muslim sects was the Moorish Science Temple Divine and National Movement of North America (later known as the Moorish Temple of Science). It was founded in Newark, New Jersey by Noble Drew Ali (Timothy Drew) in 1913. Drew Ali taught that Allah had ordained him as his prophet to the dark people of America. Ali also taught that African-Americans would find salvation and empowerment by discovering their true identity and refusing to be called Negro, Black, colored, Ethiopian, etc. He suggested "Asiatic," "Moor" or "Moorish-American" as the appropriate title for those of African descent.

The theme of empowerment was a central concern for the Black nationalist Islamic sects which trace their roots back to the Moorish Temple of Science. The issues of dignity, identity and divine significance were at the heart of their theologies.

Noble Drew Ali died in 1929. The following year, W.D. Fard, claiming to be the reincarnation of Noble Drew Ali, founded the Temple of Islam. From this organization came the "Lost, Found Nation of Islam in the Wilderness of North America," founded by Elijah Muhammad in 1933. The name of the sect was later shortened to the "Nation of Islam."[5]

Calypso Gene

Although Louis Farrakhan gets considerable media attention, the overwhelming majority of African-American Muslims are "mainline" Muslims and do not follow him.[6] However, most of these orthodox Muslims were introduced to Islam through Elijah Muhammad's Nation of Islam, Farrakhan's Nation of Islam or some similar group.

Louis Abdul Farrakhan was born Louis Eugene Walcott on May 11, 1933, in New York City. As a young man he became an accomplished musician, learning the guitar and the violin. He also displayed outstanding skills as an orator. In the early 1950s he enrolled at Winston-Salem Teachers College in North Carolina, but he did not graduate. Because he was a gifted preacher, his studies faded into the background as the demand for his ministry increased.

Walcott eventually moved to Boston, Massachusetts, where he became a guitar-playing calypso singer calling himself "Calypso Gene." Even during this time, his lyrics were more concerned with politics and social issues than with love and relationships. While he was an entertainer, Walcott was recruited into the Nation of Islam by Malcolm X. After his conversion to Islam he adopted the name Louis X, and later Elijah Muhammad gave him the name Louis Abdul Farrakhan.

Farrakhan worked closely with Elijah Muhammad and quickly rose through the ranks. By 1963 he had become chief minister of Temple No. 11 in Boston. When Malcolm X broke with Elijah Muhammad and left the Nation of Islam, Farrakhan succeeded him as chief minister of Temple No. 7 in New York City's Harlem district. In 1972 Elijah Muhammad named Farrakhan national spokesman for the Nation, another position once held by Malcolm X.[7]

Factions

Warith Deen Muhammad (then called Wallace D.), son of Elijah Muhammad, had left the Nation of Islam along with Malcolm X. But after the assassination of Malcolm, Warith returned to the Nation in 1969. His father restored him to the ministry in 1974. In 1975, Elijah Muhammad died of congestive heart failure. The following day the Nation of Islam pronounced Warith Deen the new leader. Under his leadership, the organization was transformed into an orthodox community of American Sunni Muslims. Several reactionary factions resisted the changes and held to the doctrines of Elijah Muhammad. Louis Farrakhan led one of these factions.

He broke with Deen Muhammad in December 1977 and founded the "Original Nation of Islam" (now known simply as the Nation of Islam). Others broke with Warith Deen during this time, including Silas Muhammad, who founded the "Lost, Found Nation of Islam" in 1976; John Muhammad, who founded another group called "Nation of Islam" in 1978; *Caliph* Emanuel Muhammad, who founded yet another group called the "Nation of Islam" in 1978; and Solomon X, who emerged from obscurity in the mid-1990s as "Solomon, Allah in person." He founded the "United Nation of Islam" in 1997.

Universal Theology?

With the eruption of World War I, European immigration had virtually halted while the demand for labor in the industrial North dramatically increased. Thus began the great African-American migrations from the rural South to the urban North in search of jobs and an escape from poverty.

Had the theology of empowerment fully developed, it would have been an ideal basis for the church's involvement in the Northern urbanized African-American community. But the African-American church never completely recovered from the effects of the three major traumas of the previous century. The theology of suffering was unable to address Northern urban issues. Thus, without an adequate theological base, the involvement of African-American Christians tended to be *sociological,* not theological. When the Nation of Islam emerged, thousands eagerly embraced the organization's theology of empowerment and identity along with its mythology explaining White racist behavior.

Under Elijah Muhammad, the Nation of Islam was belligerent toward the church. Not knowing the history of the African-American church, they saw Christianity as the "White man's religion"—a tool for pacifying Black people and accommodating them to their oppression. When Malcolm X, Stokely Carmichael and others popularized the message of identity and empowerment, an anti-Christian consensus developed among the militants who embraced these ideas. They saw the need to de-Christianize African-American culture in order to make progress. Because secularism proved to be a dismal failure as a base for de-Christianization, orthodox Islam became the theological base of choice.

But this posed some serious problems. Contrary to the myth that Islam is indigenous to Africa, the very essence of the religion is exclusively rooted in

Arab language and culture. Thus orthodox Islam
and American Black culture would have to function
in an "oil and water" relationship.

The Black Muslims eventually wanted to replace
this unstable dualism with a solid theological and
cultural unity. Some tried. But to do this, they had
to absolutize Islam *or* African-American culture.
Because oil and water cannot blend, neither
method brought success. In the mid-1970s some Islamic thinkers took the approach of Warith Deen
Muhammad, who had seen that Islam would never
dislodge the African-American church. He reluc-
tantly began to concede to the church a minor role
as part of a general Black belief system. He was
moving toward a Black religious synthesis—a far cry
from his father's position.

In Warith Muhammad's view, neither the theology of the African-American church (expressed in
its oral tradition) nor the beliefs of the Nation of
Islam (expressed in the doctrinaire ideology of
Elijah Muhammad) were key to understanding
African-American culture. Rather, both were
merely *products* of African-American culture. As
such they could merge. This is why, for instance,
at Mosque No. 2 in Chicago, gospel choirs were
invited to sing after the Islamic services. Such a
combination of traditions at the time was the only
hope Islamic believers had to establish a place in
the African-American cultural fabric. By appealing to a proposed "universal theology," Muslims
attempted to win African-American churchgoers
to Islam.

Warith Muhammad eventually gave up on the idea of a universal theology. As a result, he led the former Nation of Islam into the Sunni Muslim orbit. For Farrakhan, this was a departure from the "true faith." That is why he broke with Warith in 1977 and founded the Original Nation of Islam, reinstating and revising Elijah Muhammad's doctrines and myths.

In the minds of many, Farrakhan has eclipsed Warith Muhammad, capturing abundant media attention with his controversial statements. By the early 1990s Farrakhan himself was appealing to the old concept of a universal theology.

Farrakhan's theological scheme has a dual-layered structure—a "water layer," which he wants the public to see, and an "oil layer" which only he sees. In the water layer is his version of a universal theology, consisting of a mystical mingling of the oral tradition of the African-American church, the doctrine of the old Nation of Islam, orthodox Islam and ancestor worship. This is why he can 1) preach like a "born again" Christian in a church context; 2) claim to be the representative of the Honorable Elijah Muhammad in a Nation of Islam context; 3) recite the *Shahada* in Arabic in an orthodox Muslim context; and 4) describe in great detail his 1985 consultation with the late Elijah Muhammad and Master Fard Muhammad ("Allah in the flesh") on board the "Mother Ship" (a flying saucer or "wheel," which is presently circling the earth).

The "oil layer" is the Neo-Nation of Islam. He

himself is the embodiment and fulfillment of this form of Islam-ism.[8]

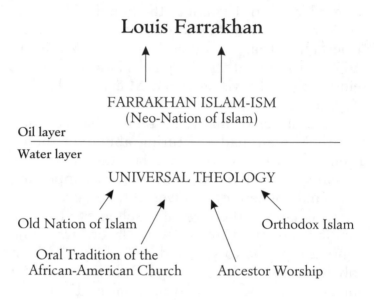

In his speeches, Farrakhan makes a sharp distinction between historic figures and prophetic figures. For example, the historic Elijah, Jesus and Muhammad prefigured and pointed to their prophetic fulfillment—the Honorable Elijah Muhammad—the long-awaited "Messiah." In 1975, Louis Farrakhan proclaimed that the late Elijah Muhammad had risen up in him. In essence, *Farrakhan not only claims to be Elijah Muhammad's representative, he claims to be his resurrection—the second "Messiah."*

Thus far when Farrakhan speaks, he continues to quote the Bible far more than the Qur'an. In reality, it is not his brand of Islam-ism[9] or his proposed universal theology that makes his message so alluring. It is essentially "borrowed capital" from biblical truth—truth that the church has largely neglected for the past 100 years.[10]

Cultural Influence

Cultural and economic empowerment are still major concerns among the African-Americans. The core cultural issues of identity, dignity and divine global significance are still contemporary. Malcolm X and the Nation of Islam both built their reputations by addressing these issues. Today three additional issues are high on the African-American cultural agenda. They are *pain, rage* and a *quest for true masculinity.*

One recent unfortunate development has been the division of the African-American community into a largely successful middle class and an underclass with virtually no chance of "making it." Middle-class Black Americans have much more in common with middle-class Whites than with the Black underclass. Many work for Fortune 500 companies, reside in affluent and sometimes integrated neighborhoods and generally live well.

Yet there is a well-documented African-American sense of alienation—a feeling of exclusion from mainline America. From the glass ceiling in the corporate world to the "good old boy" network in the South, the American system has conveyed the feeling that no matter how successful you are, the American mainstream will never fully accept you.

Because of this sense of alienation, many African-Americans tend to see Whites as working together by design and Blacks working individually and often querulously. This is behind the characterization of White America as "the Man"—the all-powerful, ubiquitous "system." Despite the apparent success of an increasing number of African-Americans, a rage persists against a system they perceive as restrictive and racist.

In brilliantly crafted rhetoric, Louis Farrakhan articulates this alienation and rage. For this reason, a sizable slice of the middle-class African-American community admires him. They would never dream of joining the Nation of Islam, yet they see Farrakhan as standing up to the system and not being intimidated.

Within the underclass, the alienation is many times more intense. The isolation they feel exacerbates their sense of alienation—isolation not only from mainstream America, but from the African-American middle class as well. The Black underclass still suffers from racism, classism and segregation. They never saw any real benefit from the Civil Rights or Black Consciousness Movements.

The institutions that were supposed to help the underclass have basically failed. Instead of breaking the cycle of poverty, these institutions have tended to confine underclass culture to the ghetto.

This failure is significant because most members of the Nation of Islam come from the ranks of the underclass. Their attraction to the Nation is driven by their desire to explain their economic deprivation and social disorganization.

Farrakhan not only articulates the rage of the underclass, but he also gives reasons for their sense of pain.

"True Masculinity"

It is not just members of the underclass in general whom the Nation attracts. Most of its members have been recruited from the church—another distinct dimension to the profile of the African-American Muslim. What does Islam provide that American Christianity does not? The answer is found in one of the great debates of contemporary society concerning the status and future of the Black male, called by some an "endangered species." One of Louis Farrakhan's major themes is the need for men to be men. Because of this, he is perceived as the champion of issues related to the quest for true masculinity.

When young male members of the Nation are asked why they prefer Islam over Christianity, they often say things like, "Christianity is too female," or "It's a religion for punks." Clearly, they perceive the church as "Black male unfriendly." This impression is attributable to the all-too-common effeminate White images of Jesus and the absence of active young men in the church.

Even the church is described in feminine terms. Such paradigms may be biblical and legitimate. It does not follow, however, that they are appropriate in all cultural situations. For example, the New Testament calls the church the bride of Christ. This is a difficult concept for young men in the 'hood trying to come to terms with their manhood. In contrast, the Nation of Islam's ethos of a warrior elite (e.g., the "Fruit of Islam") has much greater appeal.

The Bible also describes the Church as a cadre of warriors (1 Corinthians 9:26, 2 Corinthians

10:4, Ephesians 6:12, 1 Timothy 1:18 and 6:12, and 2 Timothy 4:7), but such passages are rarely emphasized. Perhaps African-American men would have better understood the Church's message if it had been couched in the "warrior" paradigm.

The March

As the 1990s dawned, it was obvious that the next phase in the African-American struggle against oppression had to be spiritual. But the church continued to stay within the bounds of its traditional concerns—and consequently missed a golden opportunity to shape the next phase of the African-American struggle.

Louis Farrakhan sensed this vacuum and sought to fill it. Late in 1994 he began to call for a million African-American men to march on Washington, D.C. on October 16, 1995. The march was billed as "a day of atonement and reconciliation" when African-American men were to "atone for their sins" such as absentee fatherhood and disrespect for women. The theme of the march was taken from Second Chronicles 7:14:

> If my people, who are called by my name, will humble themselves and pray and seek my face and turn from their wicked ways, then will I hear from heaven and will forgive their sin and will heal their land.

It was also a day for African-American men to "reconcile themselves to God." Women were encouraged to support the men by staying home. The positive atmosphere of the orderly march profoundly affected all who attended.

The response to his call was outstanding. The National Park Service estimated the attendance at 400,000, but researchers from Boston University, using digital technology, estimated the crowd at 870,000. More than sixty percent of the participants clearly identified themselves as Christians. The terms "atonement" and "reconciliation" as well as the theme verse are near the hearts of many Christians.

On that day, Farrakhan's rambling speech lasted two hours and twenty minutes. (By comparison, Martin Luther King, Jr.'s "I Have a Dream" speech lasted only nineteen minutes.) Farrakhan likened himself to a prophet God was using to call African-Americans together. He may have intended it to be a kind of coronation, but the march itself developed a synergy of its own. "This isn't a *Farrakhan* thing, it's a *Black* thing!" was a statement frequently heard among the participants.

After the march, hundreds of thousands of African-American men made moral resolutions to improve their lives. It was apparent that God's Spirit had moved on African-American men across the United States to "hunger and thirst for righteousness."

Farrakhan's message served as a wake-up call for the church to rediscover the fullness of the gospel in contemporary issues. Several African-American evangelical leaders across the United States hastily called meetings and organized forums to discuss the Christian response to the March. Most suggestions were within the traditional parameters of evangelical concern. Few, if any, realized that these parameters are inadequate to deal with mainstream African-American core cultural issues.[11]

This is to be expected, since the evangelical agenda has never connected with historic African-American issues such as dignity, identity and the divine significance of the Black experience. Neither does today's evangelical agenda address deeply felt issues of rage and pain.

The quest for true masculinity has emerged as a major concern in movements such as Promise Keepers. For this we can praise God. However, it is unfortunate that Promise Keepers as an evangelical movement, in spite of its attempts to reach out to African-Americans, has inherited a legacy it does not want and did not create: evangelicalism's perceived cavalier attitude toward racism. Thus when Promise Keepers called men to become genuine men by standing for righteousness, the negative reputation of evangelicalism overpowered the message for many African-Americans.

In contrast, although Farrakhan's message was fraught with racist overtones and innuendoes, for many Blacks it came through much more clearly than the evangelical voice. When Farrakhan's call went out for a "day of atonement and reconciliation," it resonated with African-American men's God-given desire for righteousness.

It is not enough for the African-American church to rest on its past successes. It has historically been the strongest institution in the African-American community. But that has not prevented and will not prevent the church from being in a state of decline.

There is the potential for a great harvest among those involved in the Nation of Islam if the church takes Farrakhan's challenge seriously—if we address the African-American desire for righteousness and empowerment biblically. But if the church fails to take this challenge seriously, then the Muslim presence will become a Muslim dominance and a scourge upon the church.

Notes

1 The Emancipation Proclamation was issued by President Abraham Lincoln on September 22, 1862. It took effect on January 1, 1863. However, slavery continued in many areas of the South until the ratification of the Thirteenth Amendment on December 18, 1865.

2 Carl F. Ellis, Jr., *Free at Last* (Downers Grove, IL: InterVarsity Press, 1996), 219-220.

3 The Thirteenth, Fourteenth and Fifteenth Amendments to the U.S. Constitution were largely concerned with the Constitutional status of the newly freed slaves.

   The Thirteenth Amendment (ratified on December 18, 1865) buttressed the Emancipation Proclamation of 1863. It extended the abolition of slavery to the North and West as well as the South.

   The Fourteenth Amendment (ratified on July 28, 1868) proclaimed that the former slaves were full citizens of the United States, entitled to civil rights and due process of law.

   The Fifteenth Amendment (ratified on March 30, 1870) forbade any state from depriving its Black citizens of the right to vote because of their race or their former status as slaves.

4 Ellis, 54.

5 Other groups that trace their roots to the Moorish Temple of Science are The Moorish Science Temple Divine and National Movement of North America, founded by Grand Sheik Richardson Dingle-El in 1975, and the Five Percent Nation of Islam, founded by Clarence 13X in 1964. The Nubian Islamic Hebrews (also known as the Ansari Community, the Tents of Kedar and the Tents of Abraham) also advocate empowerment through

identity. This group, however, did not directly emerge from the Moorish Temple of Science.

6   One of the newest and most radical of Black separatist Islamic groups was founded by Khallid Abdul Muhammad, the former national spokesman for Louis Farrakhan's Nation of Islam.

On November 19, 1993, Khallid delivered an inflammatory speech at Kean College (now Keen University) in Union, NJ. Because this speech aroused such a vitriolic national outrage, Farrakhan ousted Khallid from the Nation. Soon afterward, Khallid founded the New Black Muslim movement.

The American Muslim Mission is by far the largest mainline African-American Muslim group. Other "orthodox Muslims" include the Al-Hanif; Hanafi Madh-Hab Center; Islam Faith, United States of America; American Mussulmans; and the Ahmadiyya Movement, USA. There are also a few Shi'ites and Sufis among African-Americans.

7   Ellis, 225-226.

8   Ibid., 123-126.

9   This hyphenated form "Islam-ism," is used to distinguish it from "Islamism." "Islamism" most often refers to radical Islamic fundamentalists, known for their hatred of non-Muslims and for their use of terrorism. "Islam-ism" simply refers to non-Islamic religious beliefs and practices expressed in the language of Islam, e.g., the Black nationalist-oriented Muslim sects.

10 Ellis, 125.

11 Ibid., 249-251.

Part 3

The Bible and Islam

8

The Bible vs. the Qur'an

In Parts 1 and 2 we looked at Islam in America and developed profiles of the various kinds of Muslims who live in the West. For Christians, a major question arises concerning how we should view the adherents of Islam, be they offensive-activists or defensive-pacifists. What is their actual spiritual state? How does the God of the Bible view them?

How Christians Look at World Religions

1. Creations of Satan

Historically, Christians have viewed adherents of the major world religions in several ways. Some have considered these philosophies to be creations of Satan, who, as we know from the Bible, is bent upon deceiving as many individuals as possible and keeping them from a true knowledge of God. Those who hold to this position maintain that the precepts of Islam and other religions fall under the "doctrines of demons" which the Apostle Paul speaks of in First Timothy 4:1.

2. Human sinfulness

Others, however, claim that while Satan and his demons may indeed have played a role in establishing the non-Christian religions, blame for their continued development should actually be placed at the door of human sinfulness. In the first chapter of Romans, Paul explains that knowledge of the One True God is available to all humans through His created works. But all have perverted and twisted this knowledge, forming alternative systems of religion which are mockeries of true faith.

3. Human longing for God

A third group takes a "softer" approach, claiming that religions of the world come from a longing for God which exists in every human being by virtue of the common grace which God dispenses to all. This innate desire leads many people to abandon worldly pursuits in order to seek after God. Those who maintain this view believe that only Christianity contains the completeness of revelation for a full and saving knowledge of God, but the existence of other religious systems is evidence that many persons are "doing the best they can with the knowledge they have."

4. Preparation for the gospel

Others go even further than this, claiming that the non-Christian religions are being used by God as "preparations for the gospel." In other words,

God has allowed various tribes and people groups to retain legends and myths which contain spiritual truths handed down from the earliest years of the human race. Christian missionaries are able to use these narratives as starting points to present the gospel message, explaining how such stories find their fulfillment in the person and work of Jesus the Christ.

5. Different paths to God

Finally, a fifth group has proposed that the major world religions are alternative paths to God. They are admittedly quite different from the Christian faith but nonetheless in their own right; they lead various peoples to knowledge of the One True God through different cultural means. Thus the Jewish and Christian God Yahweh, the Muslim Allah, the Hindu Brahman and the Chinese Shang-Ti are only different names for the same divine being.

Which of these views is correct? Or can there be more than one correct perspective?

One's position depends essentially upon one's view and interpretation of the Bible. It is the author's view that the Bible as we have it is "God-breathed," to use the words of Paul (2 Timothy 3:16). It is wholly inspired by God and without error in all that it affirms and teaches. God inspired the writers of the various biblical texts, and their communication is to be understood literally from the context in which they wrote. Furthermore, the essence of the Bible's teaching is to be applied in all times and in all places by all peoples.

Other Religions in the Bible

The Bible only speaks of non-Christian religions in a negative sense. The very first of the Ten Commandments forbids the worship of any god other than the One True God. The existence of other spiritual beings with supernatural powers and abilities who might be worshiped is nowhere denied, but human contact with them is forbidden. The Bible names several of these false gods, as well as the punishment for involving oneself in their worship.

Baal, for instance, was a god of the sun. When God's people, the Israelites, turned aside to worship Baal, this provoked God to anger. He handed over the Israelites to raiders who sacked and ruined their cities (see Judges 2:12-15). Baal worship sometimes led to the sacrifice of sons and daughters in fire, a practice for which the death penalty was commanded in ancient Israel (see 2 Kings 17:16-17 and Leviticus 20:1-2). Worshiping Baal often included receiving alleged revelations from him, information which according to God's prophets should be considered completely false (see Jeremiah 23:13).

The Bible portrays Baal worship as behavior which could eventually become compulsive; "running after the Baals" was equated with wild, uncontrollable lust. "It's no use!" Jeremiah quotes one such worshiper. "I love foreign gods, and I must go after them!" (see Jeremiah 2:25). For these reasons, God commanded the destruction of altars to Baal (Judges 6:25) and at several points in Israel's history, the priests of Baal and all his worshipers were executed (see 1 Kings 18:40 and 2 Kings 10:18-25).

Other gods and goddesses mentioned in the Bible include Ashtoreth (2 Kings 23:13), Molech (1
Kings 11:5-7 and Leviticus 20:1-5), Marduk, Bel
and Nebo of the Babylonians (Isaiah 46:1 and Jeremiah 50:2), Chemosh of the Moabites (1 Kings
11:33) and Rephan (Acts 7:43).

Other Religions in the World Today

The above list, of course, contains only the false deities mentioned in the Bible. Literally tens of thousands of other such gods are named in other religions,
from Lat, Uzza and Manat of the pre-Islamic Arabs
(see Sura 53:19-20 of the Qur'an), to the Hindu
Brahma, Vishnu and Shiva, and the avatars of Vishnu
such as Rama, Krishna and others. One can speak of
the Manushi and Dhyani Buddhas and the Bodhisatt-
vas of Mahayana Buddhism, and the *kami* spirits of
Japan. The Amesha Spentas of Zoroastrianism and
the thousands of spirits associated with the world's
primal religions join the list. Who—or what—are
these deities? Only three explanations are possible.

1. Real gods

The spiritual beings worshiped by the adherents
of non-Christian religions are actually gods and
goddesses in the sense of uncreated, eternal, self-
existent and all-powerful entities.

But if this explanation is true, then biblical revelation—which claims that Yahweh is the One True
God—is false and must be discounted. If even a single deity worshiped by the adherents of a non-
Christian religion is an uncreated, self-existent being, then Christianity is a false religion, for the Bible

claims to be the exclusive revelation of the One True God. This would mean that the religious system with the greatest number of adherents today and the longest continuous existence (considering its roots in Old Testament Judaism) has no basis in fact and is only a delusion.

2. Human imagination

The multiple gods and goddesses seen in polytheistic religions are merely the fantastic creations of human imagination. According to this view, popular among anthropologists and psychologists of religion, humans have observed various natural forces and have "recognized" in these forces personal traits. They have then endowed these powers with purpose and will and have assigned them gender and names.

While this alternative is perhaps more believable than the first, it has several problems. One of the most significant is that the number of gods and goddesses of the world's religions far exceeds the possible categories of natural forces. Various groups of people could "invent" gods or goddesses personifying the sun, moon, wind, fire, lightning and the like, but it becomes difficult to explain the multiplicity of gods found in folk Hinduism, Mahayana Buddhism, Native American shamanism, the Aryan religions and ancient Japanese and Chinese religions. The gods and goddesses of these systems greatly outnumber the variety of natural forces known to be in existence.[1] Even assigning each "cosmic force" a series of "relatives" fails to explain the enormous number of designated beings.

3. Demonic angels

The multiplicity of gods and goddesses in history and in contemporary world religions are demonic, the fallen angels spoken of in the Bible as the followers of Satan in his rebellion against God.

The Bible indicates that angels are an order of creation separate from human beings. They are "ministering spirits" who have great powers (Hebrews 1:14). They can appear in human form (John 20:12 with Luke 24:4). They exist in hierarchies (witness the existence of "archangels," such as Michael in Jude 9), and they were created to serve God Himself (Psalm 91:11).

But one of these angels, who many consider to have been an archangel in charge of the earth (Ezekiel 28:14), refused to serve and led a cosmic rebellion against his creator, the One True God. Apparently a large number of angels followed him in his rebellion, so now there are two separate categories of angelic beings. One category continues as servants of the One True God, while the other has become His ruthless opponents (Matthew 25:41).

Each group exercises influence over the human race. The elect angels do so only in accordance with the plan of God. In no case do they usurp the autonomy of human beings by "possessing" them; neither do they assume autonomy of their own. The followers of Satan, on the other hand—now called demons—appear to connive with Satan to deceive humans and keep them from the knowledge of God. They use a variety of means. One means usurps human autonomy through "demon possession" or "demonization," in which individual humans come under the direct control of one or more of these angelic beings. Such humans may then speak words or perform acts of essentially demonic origin.

Many believe—including this author—that such a strategy has given rise to the non-Christian religions of the world. Through direct possession or direct inspiration (or both), humans have become witting or unwitting agents of satanic inspiration and have consequently given rise to deceptive beliefs and practices. The purpose is to distract men and women from true knowledge of God, to trap them in an alternative religious system and lull them into a false sense of spiritual security.

Angels in general are known to be numerous; Revelation 5:11 records the number around the throne of God as "thousands upon thousands, and ten thousand times ten thousand."

While the number which originally followed Satan in his rebellion is uncertain, some Bible scholars have speculated that Revelation 12:4 indicates that a third of them were drawn after him. Some of these demonic angels are apparently confined in the Abyss (Greek *Tartarus*) until the day of judgment (2 Peter 2:4 and Jude 6). But indications are that a large number remain free and employ their angelic powers for evil purposes.

One account of demonic possession in the Gospels reveals that demons inhabiting a single human being were equivalent to a Roman legion, or some 6,000 individuals (Mark 5:9). Even if the demons within the man exaggerated their numerical strength, note that the demons entered a herd of 2,000 pigs (5:13). It appears that the population of demons is large, and their nature would desire to present themselves as gods and goddesses. They are in league with Satan, who aspired to be exalted like God (Isaiah 14:13-14; Ezekiel 28:15-18) and worshiped by Jesus Himself (Matthew 4:9). It is certainly plausible that his minions have similar goals.

In several passages in both the Old and New Testaments, the idolatrous gods of biblical peoples are either equated or closely connected with demons or demonic activity. Moses, for example, recorded in Deuteronomy that the Israelites, in their apostasy, were offering sacrifices to demons (Deuteronomy 32:15-17). This claim is repeated in Psalm 106:34-38, which states that Israelites were actually offering their sons and daughters to demons as sacrifices. And the Apostle Paul claims that while pagans believe they are offering sacrifices to God, they are actually offering them to demons (1 Corinthians 10:19-21).

It is thus biblically justifiable to propose that *all* of the "deities" and "spirits" which are worshiped around the world by billions of persons are actually demons who are exercising the maximum amount of power God allows them. Their objectives are multiple: Pride and arrogance drive them to demand and receive worship; their sensuality craves the pleasures of inhabiting a physical body; their depravity delights in leading human beings into sinful practices, and their deceitfulness derives satisfaction from keeping persons from the light and knowledge of the One True God.

"Angelic" Visits

In nearly all religious systems, spirit beings are believed to have contacted humans. Vedic Hinduism teaches about the *devas* (literally "the shining ones"), who were influential in the earliest years of the religion. Japanese Shinto speaks of the *kami* spirits, who play a similar role. Among groups that call themselves Christian, Joseph Smith claimed to found the Church of Jesus Christ of Latter-Day Saints on the basis of an angel's revelation, as did Ellen White in her establishment of the Seventh Day Adventist Church.

Similarly, all Muslims acknowledge that the origin of Islam may be traced to the influence of an angelic being upon Muhammad. Who was this angel? He claimed to be Gabriel, the angel who had spoken to Mary about the birth of Jesus. But in reading the Qur'an, which contains the angel's revelations, we find that his teachings diametrically opposed the most fundamental doctrines of the Christian faith (i.e., the crucifixion and resurrection of Jesus, His substitutionary atonement for the sins of mankind, His divinity and the necessity of submission to His Lordship).

Christians, who start from the presupposition that the Bible is true, have no choice but to conclude that the angel seen and heard by Muhammad must have been a fallen angel, a minion of Satan. Consequently the Qur'an, dictated by this angel, and the *hadith*, which record the practices of Muhammad based on the angel's revelations, are revealed as false teachings.

It grieves me deeply to make such statements, for I know that they are hurtful to many Muslims whom I count as friends. And since even the Bible records that God sometimes uses angels to make announcements to humans, I understand why they are puzzled—and in some cases angered—that Christians are reluctant to receive the angel's revelation given to Muhammad. This is certainly a fair question: Why *do* Christians not believe in the revelation given to the founder of Islam? For the remainder of the chapter we will focus on the question.

Why Christians Reject Muhammad's "Revelation"

1. Satan appears as an "angel of light."

The Bible warns that Satan himself may appear to humans as an "angel of light" (2 Corinthians 11:14). Many interpreters of Ezekiel 28:11-18 believe that while this passage addressed in the first person the king of Tyre during the lifetime of Ezekiel, the satanic power which apparently guided him was addressed as well. It is certain that the king of Tyre, living in the sixth century B.C., had not been "in Eden" (28:13), and thus the passage moves beyond a literal level to a spiritual level as well.

If indeed the person of Satan is addressed here, he is not described in medieval fashion as a flaming red being with horns, goat's feet and pitchfork. He is instead depicted as the most beautiful of all of God's creations—"the model of perfection, full of wisdom and perfect in beauty" (28:12). This description accords well with the words of Paul mentioned above: "And no wonder, for Satan himself masquerades as an angel of light" (2 Corinthians 11:14). Satan apparently still presents himself in the beautiful and perfect form in which he was originally created; he is able to take on an awesome appearance.

Paul forewarns us: angels, like Satan, can appear to people, but their beauty and seeming wisdom do not indicate their purpose and motive. We are to be on guard against such appearances. Obviously this does not mean that any and all angelic incursions into the human sphere fall into the demonic category, for we find in the Bible many accounts of angels acting as messengers of the One True God to men and women. But Paul warns us to be discerning. We are not automatically to assume that angelic appearances or angelic revelations are of God.

Consider, for instance, the manner in which the Muslim Jibril (Gabriel) operated. The angel seen by Muhammad appeared as a giant stretching from "the horizon to the sky." The biblical Gabriel was man-sized, able to stand in the confines of an enclosed Temple room (Luke 1:11). Muhammad's angel apparently inhabited desert places, for Muhammad encountered him in the cave of Hira in a mountain wilderness. In the Bible Gabriel appeared by the altar of incense in the Holy Place of the Israelite Temple and in Mary's home (1:26).

The Gabriel of the Bible delivered brief, succinct messages from God to Zechariah and Mary, and in no sense could these messages be considered theological or legal treatises. Muhammad's angel, on the other hand, recited long passages of teaching and forced Muhammad to memorize and repeat those passages to others. The biblical Gabriel delivered positive, joyous news from God, whereas the messages to Muhammad were filled with stern warnings of judgment.

In comparing the two representations of the angel Gabriel, undeniable differences result. Therefore Christians have no logical choice other than to conclude that while Muhammad may indeed have been a sincere seeker after God and in many respects led an exemplary life, the tragic truth is that he was deceived by a satanic angel.

2. The Bible is the complete message to man.

Paul warns Christians that the gospel message he and the other apostles preached—the message recorded in the book we know as the Bible—is God's *complete* and *only* message to mankind. In Galatians 1:8 Paul writes: "But even if we or an angel from heaven should preach a gospel other than the one we preached to you, let him be eternally condemned!" Anyone—human or angel—who brings a message which varies from the original gospel is to be accursed. Any message from an angel must be measured against the original revelation given by the Christian apostles. *If such a message varies at all from apostolic teaching, it is to be condemned and rejected.*

Following are some of the most significant ways that Islam differs from Christianity.

Major Differences between Islam and Christianity

1. The Holy Book

Christians believe that the Bible is the inspired Word of God and the only means for determining spiritual truth; Muslims believe that the Qur'an represents the only trustworthy revelation of God existing today. It must be emphasized that *all other differences between the two religions actually stem from this one.* What is the correct source of revealed truth?

Muslims look to the Qur'an and the traditions (*hadith*) concerning Muhammad for the precepts of their faith and practice, whereas Christians look to the Bible. Muslims believe that the Old and New Testaments *originally* contained the words of God, but were corrupted by the "vested interests" of the Jews and Christians. The Jews, for instance, recognized that they were descended from Abraham's *second* son, Isaac, and that Middle Eastern customs give the inheritance of the father—including possessions and property—to the *firstborn* son. For Abraham, this was Ishmael, from whom the Muslims claim to be descended.

Islam teaches that the Muslim peoples are heirs to the promises made to Abraham, including possession of the land of Palestine. But for personal gain, the Jewish people concocted a far-fetched story in which Isaac becomes Abraham's heir and Ishmael and his descendants become outcasts. Members of the nation of Israel, it is said, have added this story to the historical documents as justification for Israel's actions throughout ancient history. In the contemporary world, Muslims use this argument to address the Palestinian issue. What may appear to be merely theological trivia has very practical—even deadly—consequences in the areas of politics and culture.

With regard to the New Testament, Muslims believe that Jesus never indicated that He was God or a member of a Triune God. He presented Himself only as the Son of Man—a human being—and was no more than the great prophet which Muslims call Him. They believe that Christians were not satisfied to portray Jesus as a man and chose to deify Him. Thus they concocted the idea of the Trinity. For the Muslim, the Trinitarian doctrine is blasphemous, since it represents a fundamental contradiction of both the biblical and quranic claims that God is one. The idea of a Triune God is said to be polytheistic and a denial of very clear tenets in both the Jewish and Muslim scriptures.

Muslims believe that passages traditionally interpreted to indicate the Deity of Jesus and the Holy Spirit were added *after* the idea of the Trinity had been developed. Or, Christians who hold to a Trinitarian position have completely misinterpreted those passages because they desire evidence for the doctrine. Christians, of course, deny all of these claims and maintain that the Bible as we have it today has not been changed and still reflects all of the truths revealed to the inspired writers.

To summarize: Muslims believe that Christians possess an altered version of what was once the Word of God, and therefore it is no longer trustworthy. Only the Qur'an contains spiritual truth. In any point in which the Qur'an and the Bible disagree, the quranic text is to be considered accurate. Muslims will almost never allow the Christian's standard introductory phrase: "The Bible says . . ." This statement carries no weight with Muslims.

2. The identity of Jesus

The teaching of the Qur'an concerning Jesus is the next major point of departure between the religions. The Qur'an teaches that:

- Jesus was not the Son of God. Sura 9:30 claims that Christians who believe this are deluded.

- Jesus was not the incarnation of God in human flesh and He was not a member of the Trinity. Sura 5:17 and 73 make it clear that Christians who believe this are guilty of blasphemy.

- Jesus was not crucified and resurrected. Sura 4:157 states unequivocally that Jesus was not crucified, but it only *appeared* that He was.

- Jesus was not in any sense an atoning sacrifice for the sins of humanity. Sura 39:7 and 40:18-20 state that no one can take on himself the sins of another and that there is no one who can intercede for human beings when they stand before Allah on the Day of Judgment.

Some "similarities"

Some Christians who have dedicated themselves to in-depth studies of Islam are tempted to see similarities between the Muslim and Christian views of

Jesus where there are none. Samuel Zwemer's *The Muslim Christ*, Geoffrey Parrinder's *Jesus in the Qur'an* and Kenneth Cragg's *Jesus and the Muslim: An Exploration* claim that Muslims know at least certain truths regarding Jesus. These authors say that Christians can expand upon these truths so that Muslims will reach a full knowledge of Jesus. But are these "shared truths" what they appear to be?

For instance, it is often pointed out that Islam, like Christianity, teaches that Jesus was virgin born. Sura 3:45-59 contains the basic teaching regarding this event, and what we find here is that according to the Qur'an, Jesus was created in Mary's womb in the same way that Adam was created from the dust of the ground. The Holy Spirit's role in the pregnancy of Mary, as well as all incarnational aspects of the birth of Jesus, are completely missing.

Other facets of the quranic portrayal are so drastically different that they border on the bizarre. Sura 19, for instance, records that Jesus was able to speak with the mind of an adult even from His cradle.

Some Christians have attempted to make much of the English translation of Sura 3:45, where the Qur'an appears to call Jesus "the Word," and thus evoke the ideas contained in the *Logos* concept of John 1. But the Arabic word *kalima* translated here as "word" is perhaps better translated "testimony" (as it is when speaking of the declaration of the Muslim creed "There is no God but Allah and Muhammad is His messenger," called the *Shahada* or the *Kalima*). In no sense does the idea of "Word" in the Qur'an communicate what John was writing in John 1; it only says that Jesus came to be a "testimony" or "to testify" concerning Allah.

My conversations with Muslims have ascertained that the followers of Islam generally believe that Jesus taught essentially the same things as Muhammad: the Oneness of God (a denial of Trinitarianism), obedience to the Laws of God, and a future resurrection and judgment.

Christians would agree that Jesus indeed taught the Oneness of God. But they believe that He also claimed for Himself the prerogatives of deity, indicating that God's Oneness actually contains a divine Threeness. He taught obedience to the laws of God but stated clearly that these laws are summed up in the directives to love God with all of one's heart, soul, mind and strength and one's neighbor as oneself. His teaching was that unless one *exceeded* the righteousness of the scribes and Pharisees—which was a law-based righteousness—one would never see the kingdom of heaven.

Lastly, Jesus did indeed teach concerning resurrection and judgment, but not in accordance with Muslim doctrine. Islam teaches that Jesus will return to earth in the future, will die a natural death and will be resurrected with all other men and women at the last day. The Bible teaches that Jesus has already undergone death and resurrection and will Himself initiate the general resurrection of mankind (see John 6:39-54). Jesus is the standard by which judgment will take place (Acts 4:12, 17:31; Romans 2:16, 10:9-10), whereas in Islam, humans are judged solely on the basis of the works they perform in life.

Sura 3:49 mentions a "sign" that was to indicate that Jesus was a Messenger of Allah. This sign turns out to be an account of Jesus breathing life into a clay figure of a bird, an incident which is not included in the works considered by Christians to be Scripture but which rather appears in non-canonical writings. The quranic narrative is characterized by the same whimsical quality as that seen in the pseudo-Christian account. The passage under discussion continues with Jesus' statement that He "was a healer of the blind and of lepers and that He could raise people from the dead."

These aspects would pass muster with the Gospel accounts. But the phrases that follow deny God's command to abrogate all dietary restrictions, as recorded in the New Testament (see Acts 10 and Romans 14). Islam continues several dietary restrictions, such as the prohibition against pork, and thus this passage accords well with quranic teaching. But these practices are definitely sub-Christian.

Some differences

Beyond these subtle differences are the larger and more well-known ones. Muslims deny that Jesus was God, for to them this would mean that there is more than one God—a denial of their basic confession (Suras 4:157; 5:17, 72, 75, 116-117; and 43:59). They also deny that He was the Son of God, for this would imply that God had sexual intercourse with Mary—a blasphemous idea.

According to Islam, Jesus was not crucified (Sura 4:157). Some Muslims believe that when the command from Pilate went to the guards to "crucify Jesus," they seized the wrong Jesus and instead crucified Barabbas (who, according to tradition, was also named "Jesus"). The "Emmaus Road" account in Luke is thus to be interpreted as Jesus of Nazareth—in disguise—fleeing from Jerusalem as quickly as possible before the error was discovered.

He was later "raised by Allah up unto Himself" (Sura 4:158). This does not refer to the Ascension, but rather to an Enochian or Elijah-like transference of His person into the presence of God without experiencing death. This reprieve is only temporary, however, since Islamic eschatology says that Jesus will die approximately forty years after His second coming. He will then ultimately experience resurrection, but only as one human among all others in the general resurrection of the Last Day.

While Muslims highly esteem Jesus as a great prophet, they generally evaluate His life and ministry as inferior to earlier prophets and Muhammad. Sura 13:38 states that Allah had designated wives and children for all of the Prophets sent before Jesus. Therefore, in this and in other areas, Jesus' life and ministry are considered to have been incomplete and quite inferior to those of Muhammad. Indeed, according to Sura 61:6, part of Jesus' "limited mission" was to announce the Messenger who would follow Him, one whose name shall be "Ahmad" (a variant of Muhammad).

For all these reasons, we conclude that the Jesus of Islam is so utterly distinct from the Lord Jesus

Christ of the New Testament that one can scarcely believe that the two accounts are of the same person. To claim that the Qur'an reveals *any* truth about Jesus stretches the limits of credibility.

3. How to attain salvation

In Islam, salvation is an external and institutional concept, a status earned through one's own merit; in biblical Christianity, salvation is internal and personal, a status conferred as an unearned and undeserved gift of God.

People become Muslims in one of two ways. For those who grow up in Muslim countries or in Muslim families, no "conversion experience" is necessary; one is simply enculturated into the religion. Males receive the sign of their status at birth through circumcision, and at appropriate times both males and females begin their participation in the prayers and other "pillars" of the Islamic religion.

For those who do not grow up in a Muslim environment, conversion occurs through a change in intellectual allegiance and ritual patterns. One simply stops believing the religion of one's parents or cultural environment and acknowledges instead the tenets of Islam. In this sense, conversion is an external process; there is no "inner change" as described by Jesus in John 3, a change so radical that He characterizes it as a "new birth."

The book of Romans and such passages as Ephesians 2:8-9 speak of salvation as being dependent upon an internal and personal faith in the person and work of Jesus Christ. But the final judgment according to Muslims will be made solely on the basis of an individual's deeds in life. The Qur'an indicates that as long as one leads a *generally good* life, one's "lapses" will be forgiven.[2]

4. Original sin

Christianity teaches that one of the consequences of the fall of Adam and Eve into sin was spiritual death and the establishment of a sinful nature in them and all their descendants. Islam teaches that human beings are not inherently sinful; they have no innately sinful nature. According to Islamic theology, all humans are born Muslims. Islam is the *din al-fitr*, the "religion of nature" or "the natural religion."

All human infants enter the world in a state of submission to God, but they are led astray by the non-Muslim cultures in which they live. Their parents bring them up to be Jews or Christians or Hindus or followers of some other false religion; if they had been left to themselves they would have automatically followed the teachings of Islam. Consequently, when a non-Muslim takes the steps to enter the religion of Islam, Muslims do not speak of that person's *conversion* but rather his or her *reversion* to the original state at birth. New Muslims are called *reverts*.

Human beings are completely on their own in the ability to do good or evil. This, of course, is consistent with the Muslim's belief that no human being can atone for the sins of another, as we saw above. Just as an individual's righteousness cannot be transferred to another, neither can another's sin be transmitted to any other.

5. Church and state

Finally, Islam advocates no separation between the state and religious institutions, but rather seeks to establish a literal "kingdom of Islam" on earth. Jesus speaks clearly of "giving to Caesar what is Caesar's, and to God what is God's" (see Matthew 22:21), and Peter speaks of the necessity of "obeying God rather than men" when faced with a situation calling for disobedience to established authority (Acts 5:29).

While the Bible advocates obedience to secular authorities and never condones direct rebellion or insurrection (Romans 13:1-5), one fails to find a preoccupation with or even involvement in the affairs of human government. The apostles concerned themselves with *internal* human affairs rather than *external* political relationships. They functioned within whatever political structure and cultural context they happened to find themselves, and did not seek to establish "Christian" political, economic, judicial or social systems.

The absence of New Testament teaching regarding these spheres of life has been problematic throughout the history of Christianity, for the desire of Christians who are imbued with biblical ideals is to change society to reflect those ideals. But since the Bible provides no practical model for the transformation of human institutions, Christian idealism as applied to the political or economic sphere has never functioned successfully within actual historical contexts—a fact with implications which we will presently discuss more thoroughly.

We live in a day devoted to ecumenism and attempts to smooth over religious differences. This is understandable in light of the religious wars that were fought in the past and which still occur in the present. But with regard to biblical Christianity and quaranic Islam, one cannot logically accept the validity of both faiths. Reconciliation of their teachings is impossible, for the gulf between the two is simply too wide to be spanned.

It cannot be that Jesus is the Son of God (as the Bible teaches) *and* that He is not the Son of God (as the Qur'an teaches). It cannot be that He was crucified and resurrected, atoning for human sin (as the Bible teaches) *and* that He was not crucified (as the Qur'an teaches). Both cannot be true—one source or the other must be wrong.

As unpopular and difficult as it may be in our postmodern world, we must chose to accept the one—and, in so doing, reject the other. The implications of such a choice will be the subject of the next chapter.

Notes

1   Noss states regarding folk Hinduism alone that "the number of these deities is uncountable. Hindus are accustomed to saying that there are thirty-three crores, some 330 million" (see David S. Noss and John B. Noss, *A History of the World's Religions,* 9th ed. [New York: Maxwell Macmillan Int., 1994], 144).

2   See Fazlur Rahman, *Major Themes of the Qur'an* (Minneapolis, MN: Bibliotheca Islamica, 1980), 30.

9

The Challenge of Islam in America

Biblical Christianity is an exclusive religion. The Word of God teaches that the Christian faith is the only avenue to reach the One True God and to obtain salvation from sin. Besides the oft-quoted verses John 14:6 and Acts 4:12, literally dozens of other passages speak of the exclusiveness of the Christian faith. If the Bible is indeed the Word of God and the sole revelation of spiritual truth, then other religions—including Islam—cannot be true. Conversely, if the other religions are true, then Christianity falsely claims to be the one true religion and most likely contains other errors as well. It is not logically possible to maintain that biblical Christianity *and* other world religions are true.

This claim is highly problematic for Christians who live in countries founded on the principles of democracy. This form of government includes the idea of *pluralism*, defined as "a theory that there is more than one basic substance or principle." In most spheres, pluralism is a perfectly acceptable and even desirable philosophy of life. Pluralistic ideals applied consistently within culture would erase racial or ethnic prejudice. Pluralism may also be said to enhance life because the availability of choices prevents stagnation and ennui.

What's a Christian to Do?

But when it comes to religious matters, Christians who literally interpret the Bible face a conflict. On the one hand, the U.S. Constitution's guarantee of the freedom of religion makes it possible to live according to one's beliefs and even to propagate those beliefs. This form of pluralism is one which every Christian should appreciate. On the other hand, the Bible's view of the world religions is anything but pluralistic. No other religion provides a way to know God or attain salvation, and therefore Christians are commanded to "make disciples of all nations." Muslims, Hindus, Buddhists, Jews and other adherents of the major world religions must be asked to give up their beliefs and rituals as they acknowledge the Lordship of Jesus Christ.

What, then, is a viable solution? Is it possible to embrace a pluralistic democracy and at the same time be a Christian exclusivist? *That duality is not only possible, but absolutely essential.* In order to implement such a paradox, we must first understand the two basic ways people relate to their God. These orientations may be termed external-institutionalism and internal-personalism. We will explore this issue in depth.

Internal Faith, External Expression

Biblical Christianity is essentially an *internal* and *personal* faith. The new birth that Jesus spoke of in John 3:1-7 takes place internally and spiritually. Nicodemus' question of how he could enter his mother's womb and be born a second time makes it clear that he was thinking in a purely physical and external sense. Jesus points out his error. The scribes and Pharisees of the first century made the same error, as do many people today. They had (and have) a difficult time understanding that true religious faith is not rituals performed in man-made institutions.

Jesus corrected the Samaritan woman at the well in John 4:4-24 because she only thought of "worship on a mountain"—a specific method in a specific place. Jesus says that ". . . true worshipers will worship the Father in spirit and truth. . . . God is spirit, and his worshipers must worship in spirit and in truth" (4:23-24).

And in Matthew 23:5 Jesus scathingly denounces the Pharisees because "Everything they do is done for men to see." They tithed, but neglected justice, mercy and faithfulness (23:23); they cleaned the outside of the cup and dish, but inside were full of greed and self-indulgence (23:25). Jesus constantly sought to redirect people from outward ritual toward inner conviction. There is no question as to Jesus' thinking with regard to the proper emphasis.

The internal and personal orientation emphasizes the need for an inner state of righteousness to "save" people. Conformity to *external* practices or rituals, be they infant baptism, confirmation, partaking of the Eucharist, service, tithing, confession to a priest, standardized prayers or church attendance, does not, according to biblical revelation, mediate the grace of God. These practices may be *expressions* of an internal state of righteousness, but they can never bring about righteousness.

Most of the Jews living in the time of Jesus had fallen into that mistake. They believed that they were righteous before God because they had descended from Abraham, and because they practiced the rituals of the Mosaic Law. While the "fruits" of one's life *may* indicate one's inner spiritual state, this is not always the case. Jesus states that it is possible to preach, cast out demons and perform miraculous works in His name and still be unrighteous (Matthew 7:21-23).

The Apostle Paul devotes much of his letter to the Romans to this very issue, and concludes that one is justified by faith—not by observing law (Romans 3:20, 28). So *no one* will attain righteousness based on beliefs or practices. The essential characteristic of true religion is *faith*. Faith is an internal *attitude* of acceptance and submission to God and a belief in what He has revealed (Romans 10:9-10).

Once this internal acceptance has occurred, faith must be expressed externally. This is what James meant when he taught that "faith without deeds is dead" (James 2:26). But acts of religious devotion are completely worthless if an internal state of faith and righteousness is not present. The tragedy of Muslims, the adherents of other non-Christian religions and even, perhaps, a majority of "Christians" is that these religious people are pursuing "righteousness" incorrectly. Literally billions of persons are lulled into a sense of false security and deceived regarding their status before God.

Many Christians *do* understand the distinction between internal-personal faith and external-institutional religious practice. They have experienced an internal and personal change of heart. They have received the gift of faith from God (Ephesians 2:8-9) and have been "born again" (John 3:1-6), acknowledging that Jesus is the Lord and Master of their lives and the resurrected, living and active Savior (Romans 10:9-10). These persons enjoy the status of being righteous before God—not because of their beliefs or practices, but because of the provision of righteousness through Jesus Christ.

Bringing about the Kingdom of God

However, many Christians who understand the distinction between external-institutionalism and internal-personalism in individual salvation do not carry it over to other matters. This brings about a number of difficulties within the Christian Church, such as radically differing views of the kingdom of God. Jesus speaks of an external and internal kingdom. After the Last Supper with His disciples, He remarks that He will not drink wine with them again until they are together in the kingdom (Luke 22:18). He speaks here of when He will establish a literal kingdom of God where He will rule as sovereign Monarch.

But when He says to His disciples that the kingdom of God is "within them" and "among them" (see Luke 17:20-21), He is speaking of the internal, personal aspects of the kingdom, particularly as it relates to our current time. Presently the kingdom is "underground," carried within and among Christians who have experienced the new birth and whose lives consistently express the Bible's principles for "kingdom living" (see the Sermon on the Mount in Matthew 5-7). So while the external and institutional aspects of the kingdom are real, they are future. The internal, personal aspects call us to concentrate *now* on living according to biblical ethics within our specific cultural contexts.

Problems arise when Christians confuse the two orientations. Many believe that the Church's task is to establish the kingdom of God institutionally so that it will provide the avenue for Jesus to return to earth. This gives an entirely different orientation than those who understand the kingdom to be only internal and personal during this time. Inevitably this confusion carries over into politics.

For those who are convinced that an institutional kingdom of God should be established here and now, questions arise. What *is* a Christian political system? How would it function? Who would lead it? What laws or principles should govern the people? And most importantly, must all of its citizens accept Christianity? If not, what requirements would exist for those who are not Christians?

Consistent "internal-personalists" are for the most part untroubled by these questions, because they are moot. *They believe Jesus left no model for a political system because Christians are to operate within whatever political structure they find themselves and make the best of whatever rights and privileges they have—few though these may be in some countries.* The goal and emphasis of these Christians is upon the internal and personal aspects of human beings, not the external institutions that sinful humans have constructed.

Does not the Bible demand, though, that Christians be "salt and light," "light of the world," "cities set on hills which cannot be hidden" (see Matthew 5:13-14)? Some Christians interpret these passages to mean that we are to influence and affect societies so as to transform them into "Christian societies." To do otherwise, they say, would allow the evil of unbelief to run rampant throughout the earth. Christians *must* speak to the issues of the day and challenge the sinful institutions of the society around us. Could we do otherwise and still be faithful to the Bible's principles?

Levels of Involvement

When dealing with external and institutional concerns, such as politics, Christians must distinguish between levels of involvement: individual, local, national and international.

Individual level

At the individual level, the Christian seeks to transform others by presenting the truth claims of

Christ, according to biblical teaching. When faith has been exercised, Jesus' lordship acknowledged and the new birth experienced, the individual begins to learn and practice Christian discipleship. This process means adopting biblical patterns which bring individual, personal change.

Local level

At the local level, individuals (usually within churches) adopt practices in keeping with the New Testament. A group may worship based on First Corinthians 14:26-35, practice common ownership of goods in accordance with Acts 2:44 and 4:32 or help widows and other needy persons as shown in First Timothy 5:3-16. It is understood that all in the group are Christians; their commitment to Christ and the Holy Spirit's work has caused internal and personal transformation leading to external changes. A few non-Christian individuals may participate, but their attempts to live a vital spiritual life without internal foundations will fail. They will reject the Christian life entirely or develop an externally oriented religious faith.

National level

At the national level difficulties begin to arise. History has never seen a nation with a majority of biblical Christians. Many nations have claimed that most of their citizens are indeed "Christians." But such claims are always based on external and institutional criteria: all of the citizens have been baptized as infants, have submitted to baptism by order of a king or some variation. Such practices do not produce biblical Christianity. In most cases, no internal change has taken place in the individual's heart and mind.

One might claim that general "Christian" principles have been the basis for the establishment of various social systems, but there is tremendous disagreement in each of these areas on the part of "Christians." We have Christian Democrats and Christian Republicans in America; Christian capitalists and Christian socialists; Christians in favor of capital punishment and Christians who vehemently oppose it; Christians in favor of abortion on demand and Christians who violently reject it. And we have, of course, Christian exclusivists and Christian pluralists.

International level

A purely "Christian"—or Muslim, Hindu, Buddhist or Jewish—nation is conceivable, at least nominally. Moral and legal precepts could be imposed upon all citizens identified as "Christian" (for the purposes of our illustration) on the basis of specific practices such as infant baptism, circumcision, etc. But internationally, the diversity of today's religious traditions would make this impossible. While "global Christianity" or "global Islam" might be the goal of some, few adherents believe it will ever be achieved.

Attempts to impose external, institutional Christianity upon Muslim, Hindu or Confucianist nations would meet with militant opposition and resistance, just as reciprocal attempts would receive from "Christian" nations. Some ecumenicists are searching for common ground among the world's religions. But cooperative activities are usually economic or social. They avoid political statements or activities and suppress all thoughts of religious conversions. At the international level, the goal of a *spiritual* transformation is almost entirely absent.

Muslims in the West

How does all of this relate to the attitude of evangelical Christians toward Muslims living in the West? To pluralism and exclusivism? Let us propose a biblical position regarding this issue.

When dealing with Muslims, Christians should function individually as exclusivists, but locally, nationally and internationally as pluralists.

This principle distinguishes between Christians dealing with Muslims in everyday living and dealing with their community, nation and world as a whole. At the local, national and international levels, the operative words for Christian activity and advocacy would be *secularization, democratization* and *pluralization*.

This proposal is perhaps startling, for "secularization" brings to mind godlessness, atheism and agnosticism without morality and with materialism. Is it permissible for Christians of biblical integrity to "secularize" nations? Should not followers of Christ attempt to *Christianize* nations? But to have a "Christian nation," one must have a model—a definable goal or end result. Is there any one *Christian* political, economic, judicial or social system? Would a "Christian society" be founded on a Roman Catholic, Eastern Orthodox, Coptic or Protestant model? Would it be Presbyterian, Anglican, Congregational, Baptist or Anabaptist? Is there hope of reaching even at the local level consensus regarding a Christian society? Christians cannot realistically expect to accomplish such a task.

Even if a majority of persons who call themselves Christians were to settle upon a "kingdom of God on earth," would it not be necessary to impose such a system upon non-Christian and nominally Christian citizens? We evangelicals hold that the "new birth" spoken of by Jesus is essential for entering the kingdom of heaven; it must be a *voluntary* and *deliberate* commitment to the lordship of Christ (Romans 10:9-10). Can we advocate a plan which undermines the voluntary? For individuals to sincerely be internally transformed, they must have freedom of choice. And only secular, democratic and pluralistic societies guarantee religious freedom, creating an open playing field for all.

An Open Society

Such a strategy involves risks. Chief of these is that a society will pursue secularization past the point of survival. Some believe that certain Western nations are already headed this way, but this end is not inevitable. Christians working through curricula, media, literature, political action committees and the like can control secularization and pluralism. And this is what evangelicals should be doing.

Making the case *directly* for Christianity at the local, national or international levels will cause immediate rejection by persons holding non- or anti-Christian sentiments. But we may lobby with integrity for a pluralistic society which guarantees the right to practice and propagate one's religious convictions. Within such a system Muslims, Hindus, Buddhists, Jews and others will be allowed to carry out missionary activity. But Christians would be guaranteed the right to continue their own evangelizing, disciple-making and church-planting efforts, which they might lose under a purely Islamic, Hindu, Buddhist or Jewish state.

A second risk: Allowing world religions to compete openly may produce "syncretism," which combines practices and/or beliefs of religious systems to form an individualistic faith. It suppresses, alters or eliminates essential elements of the contributing religions. The African "nativistic movements" are considered a classic case of syncretism.

But the African scholar Humphrey Fisher has observed that syncretism resulting from secular pluralism nearly always results in "snapping" to one extreme or the other.[1] Trying to hold Christianity together with, for instance, animistic or Islamic beliefs becomes unbearable, and adherents eventually choose to become fully Christian, fully Muslim or fully animist. Obviously there is risk here—but one that could work in the favor of Christianity.

Another major problem in advocating secularization, democratization and pluralization is that adherents of other world religions see no need for an open playing field. A secular society is incompatible with most of these religions, which have external and institutional strategies. Here Christians must distinguish between "secularization" (a social process) and "secularism" (a social philosophy),[2] and point out the problems encountered in defining a religious state. Muslims, for instance, are extremely divided over what a purely *Muslim* political, economic, social and even religious system would be, and they must understand the advantages of adopting an open playing field.

It is vitally important that Christians make clear that a secularized society does not aim to *exclude or eliminate* religious influences but to *preserve* them. While a society devoted to the philosophy of *secularism* might banish religious practices in toto, classical *secularization*—as seen in the concept of separation of church and state—seeks to preserve them. When Christians advocate secularization, democratization and pluralization, they must do so *to preserve and defend the right to choose and practice their religious beliefs*. Within these boundaries is a society which does not require—and which essentially forbids—a *forced* commitment to a specific way of salvation. Then soteriological and other differences can be presented, examined and discussed and voluntary commitments elicited.

What Individuals Can Do

Individually, however, biblical Christians must remain exclusivist. Using the freedom provided at the local, national and/or international levels, Christians who meet Muslims must boldly point out the differences between the faiths and seek to convince the Muslim of his or her need for salvation based on the gracious gift of atonement through Jesus Christ alone. The key concepts at this level are *particularistic evangelism* and *discipleship*. These concepts espouse communication of the good news of Jesus Christ to as many as possible and for those who receive His salvation, instruction in all that Jesus taught. The goal must be to transmit the gospel of Jesus to every individual or family in a way that enables them to decide to accept or reject God's grace. Christians must aim at a total *saturation* of whole populations.

Such a plan must acknowledge that Muslims, Hindus, Buddhists and others will increasingly develop their own strategies for outreach. Christian evangelism will occur in a context of competition. Evangelicals may well find themselves in encounters such as in First Kings 18 in which Elijah the Prophet challenges the priests of Baal. As Yahweh visibly displayed His power, the religious constructs of Elijah demonstrated clear superiority over the priests of Baal. In today's world, Christians may need to trust in God to work just as spectacularly.

The Muslims of America will move among our neighbors, friends and coworkers, functioning both offensively and defensively from house to house and street to street. They are free to impose their beliefs and practices on others in an external and institutional fashion. Some would see this as a severe handicap for biblical Christianity, and from an earthly perspective, it could be considered so. But this should not be of concern. The sovereign God of the universe has ordained the one true way of salvation. He has decreed in His providence that righteousness cannot be obtained externally or institutionally. We as Christians, despite the supposed handicap we work under, must be out on the playing field as well, preaching the gospel message with all the faith, power and joy that we can muster.

Notes

1   Humphrey J. Fisher, "Islam and Indigenous Tradition in Africa: Is Conversion to Islam a Continuing Process within Muslim Communities?" Paper presented at the International Symposium on Islam and Ethnicity in Africa and the Middle East at the State University of New York at Binghamton, April 25-27, 1991.

2   See Os Guinness, *The Gravedigger File* (Downers Grove, IL: InterVarsity Press, 1983), 51-55, for an explanation of the distinction between these two concepts.

Part 4

When Christians and Muslims Meet

10

Witnessing to Ethnic Muslims and Converts to Islam

Christians have not done well at winning Muslims to Christ. Some persons have been designated "apostles to Islam" (such as Ramon Lull and Samuel Zwemer), but few could be considered "experts" in that their methodology has produced large numbers of conversions. The history of evangelism among Muslims is depressing, prompting descriptions of Islam as "Satan's finest masterpiece" and "the last of the giants."

The History of Muslim Evangelism

Early in Muslim history, North African Christians, particularly Byzantine Christians, did not have much to say about Islam. As we noted in an earlier chapter, hatred of Byzantine imperialism (in particular its policies of taxation) created a situation in which Muslims were able to conquer large portions of Christendom with relative ease. The patriarch of Jerusalem, for instance, is alleged to have greeted the conqueror Umar with open arms at the gates of Jerusalem. And since Christians were allowed to retain their faith (albeit as second-class citizens), relatively peaceful coexistence was the norm throughout most of the Middle Ages.[1]

In one respect, the Crusades, which began in A.D. 1096, were the first attempt by "Christians" to deal proactively with Muslims. I am intentionally putting "Christians" in quotes, for it is highly doubtful that even a minute fraction of those on crusading expeditions were Christians in the biblical sense of the term. According to many historians, these expeditions resulted primarily from the feudal practice of primogeniture. This practice had created a surplus of young men in Europe, many of whom had no adequate means of support. Families with four or five sons did not fare well when only the oldest son inherited, and in many cases younger sons could only join the army or become highwaymen.

Pope Urban II recognized in this situation an opportunity to accomplish several goals. First, the Crusades gave the young men a mission. If they survived, they would nearly always return with enough booty to establish households of their own. If they did not return, Europe had less mouths to feed.

The Church had more or less decided that the Muslims were inhuman devils and gave no thought to bringing them to Christ. To kill them could easily be construed as service to God.

Also, Christian pilgrims who desired to visit the Holy Land—which was under Muslim rule—never felt completely secure, despite assurances that visits to Jerusalem would always be permitted. If Palestine could again become a European colony, Christians could visit the sites of Jesus' ministry without fear. But while the Crusades are understandable in their context, they have been a blight on Church history. They stamped Christianity as "the religion of the sword"—which is ironic, because Christians most often make this accusation of Islam.

The first person to implement what we would consider a truly biblical missionary strategy toward Muslims was Ramon Lull (circa 1232-1316), a resident of the Mediterranean island of Majorca who died as a martyr in North Africa. Lull was embarrassed by much of the thinking behind the Crusades, particularly that Muslims were cursed by God and therefore unsalvable. But Lull made few converts, which to many was seen as a confirmation that the traditional view of Muslims was correct.

From Lull's time until the 1800s, another huge gap in missions to Muslims appears. After the Protestant Reformation, too many issues arose for the Roman Catholic Church and new Protestant churches; expansion of the kingdom of heaven to unreached peoples became strictly secondary to maintaining territory already considered to be "Christian."[2] But the modern missionary movement of the 1800s again brought Christian missionaries to Muslim peoples, though with no better success than Lull had. Christians established schools and hospitals in Muslim lands, but attempts to communicate the gospel usually ended in failure.

Major Views of Islam

By the second quarter of the twentieth century, Christians held three major views of Islam. All were formulated out of frustration and despair that evangelism among Muslims was so incredibly unproductive. One could say that evangelical Christians in some cases developed extreme rationalizations to ease their consciences. An explanation of each of these views follows.

1. Muslims are already saved.

Since God is not seeing fit to convert Muslims, they must already be saved within their own religious faith. This view is popular among ecumenicists and those who hold a more liberal theology. These persons believe that the monotheism, adherence to a holy book and high moral standards of Islam make it a valid faith for Middle Eastern and North African peoples. They believe that the many ways to God are culturally determined.

For Asian Indians, Hinduism leads to the all-encompassing One; Brahman is just another name for God. For Southeast Asians, Buddhism accomplishes the same purpose, and for Western civilization, Christianity and Judaism point the way. For Middle Eastern peoples, Islam is the culturally appropriate path to know God. Not only is Islam not a "work of the devil," it is actually a work of God designed to bring people to Himself.

While it may indeed differ from Christianity in minor aspects, these differences only result from cultural development through the centuries.

The problem with this view is that the Bible nowhere indicates that a group of people who deny the deity, atonement, crucifixion and resurrection of Jesus can be saved by their own religious beliefs. On the contrary, the Bible makes it clear that without a total commitment to these beliefs, one cannot have a relationship with God the Father and will not attain salvation (1 John 2:23 and Romans 10:9-10).

2. God has "given Muslims over."

Since God is not seeing fit to convert Muslims, He must have given them over to their own depravity and will not save them. Some hold that certain peoples or cultures can step over a specific God-ordained line for the expansion of evil, and then He gives them over to destruction. Several Bible passages are used to support such thinking. For instance, God stated in Genesis 6:3 that His Spirit would not always continue to wrestle with individuals, which has been interpreted that God gives people only a limited number of chances to repent and turn to Him. If a people continually refuse to acknowledge His truth, He abandons them and discontinues His work in their lives and society.

Other evidence is seen in the Canaanite peoples that God ordered the Israelites to destroy completely—they were apparently no longer "salvable."[3] The Apostle Paul in his letter to the Roman church speaks of individuals who had deliberately rejected the knowledge of God and who were in turn rejected by Him (Romans 1:25-26, 28). Finally, some would hold that the Muslims' claim to be descendants of Ishmael is in itself a form of self-condemnation, for God speaks negatively of Ishmael to Abraham. He calls Ishmael a "wild donkey" and predicts enmity between him and his brothers (Genesis 16:12).

However, the Bible presents no evidence that God has "given up" on any *specific* group of people since Old Testament times. The Romans passage speaks of a certain *kind* of person—a hardened sinner—independent of whatever kind of national or religious group he or she belongs to. Certain individuals within Islam may fall into this category, but this in no way supports a conclusion that the Muslim world has already been judged. As for Paul's condemnation of Ishmael, this passage deals with the covenantal blessing, not a blanket condemnation of Ishmael and his descendants as a group of people. God's words in Genesis concerning Ishmael merely predict what he and his descendants would become; they do not pronounce a specific, irreversible destiny.

3. Muslims are not yet ready for "harvest."

Since God is not seeing fit to convert Muslims, Christian missions to the Muslim world must still be in a "seed-planting" and/or "deliverance" phase. Those who hold to this view—the only ones still actively seeking to win Muslims to Christ—believe that we as Christians must simply continue to struggle forward, planting seeds as we go. For the time being, we should not expect to see many results, since Muslim lands are "hard ground": soil not adequately prepared for the seeds of the gospel. In addition, within the last ten years or so there has been an increasing emphasis on the need to pray against or bind the demonic spirits that are said to hold sway over Muslim territories. George Otis, Jr., has written an entire book on this subject, *The Last of the Giants: Lifting the Veil on Islam and the End Times.*[4]

Otis proposes that Christians have never experienced great success in ministry to Muslims because unusually strong territorial demons blind the minds of Middle Eastern and North African peoples. Until the influence of these demons is neutralized, evangelism will not succeed among Muslim peoples. When these demonic forces are removed, God will display His power and bring in an enormous harvest. Advocates of this view remain optimistic and are still seeking to discover the proper method or strategy for missionary work among Muslims.

The author believes that according to biblical principles, evangelistic ministry to Muslims must be continued and initiated where it does not already exist. Suggestions follow for carrying out such activity.

Contextualizing the Messenger to Muslims

"Contextualization" has been a key word within missions circles for over two decades, and controversy still exists over how to define and apply this concept. In most cases, the term is used with the gospel *message* that Christians seek to communicate. "Contextualizing" means that one must modify and adapt the message so that it can be understood by the targeted audience. When dealing with Muslims, however, we need to think far more about contextualizing *ourselves* than our message. With this in mind, we will look at basic principles for adapting messengers to the lifestyle and worldview of Muslim peoples.

1. Relate to Muslims as individuals.

View, approach and deal with Muslims first and foremost as individuals, not as Muslims. Get to know them as men and women who have the same basic needs, desires, worries, joys and fears that you do.

Just as no two Christians share identical expressions of their faith, so no two Muslims are exactly the same. Think of a church service or Sunday school class—any group of Christians united in a common fellowship. They belong to the same Christian denomination, subscribe to the same creed and perform the same rituals. But a survey of beliefs regarding both Christian theology and lifestyle would reveal variations. Christians have differing levels of familiarity with the Bible. They come from a variety of backgrounds which affect their interpretation and application of the Scriptures.

The adherents of Islam are actually as individualistic as Christians, particularly Muslims in America. Sometimes we assume that a particular Muslim has beliefs that he doesn't have at all. Perhaps the individual is unaware of this part of Islamic "orthodoxy," or perhaps he disagrees with that principle or action. It is best not to interact with Muslims at the beginning of a relationship on theology or religion.

It is much better to meet them at what I call *the basic level of humanity.*

All Muslim mothers, for instance, are concerned about their children and about parenting; all Muslim fathers think about their jobs, living situations and family honor. They are concerned with the immorality of American society and the constant temptations of materialism. These are concerns of Christians as well, and one should first seek to engage Muslims in conversation concerning these kinds of topics. Let them see you as a human being in the midst of American society, dealing with the same problems and concerns. Then let them discover that you deal with those concerns on the basis of biblical principles.

Interacting in this way is good for at least two reasons. It allows the Christian to bear testimony on the practicality of his or her faith in Christ. At the same time, speaking on matters of daily living may well require more time in the Bible to learn godly principles for dealing with ethical issues.

2. Distinguish between urban and rural Muslims.

Learn to distinguish between urban and rural Muslims, since you will need to relate to these persons in different ways. The typical American will usually experience greater cultural and religious dissonance with persons from rural rather than urban environments.

Generally speaking, there are major differences between persons who have come from Middle Eastern or North African cities and those who have come from rural environments. Recall that some of the earlier immigrants from Muslim countries came from rural areas with poor living conditions and difficult employment. Many of these immigrants have continued in America their basic approach to life from their home countries.

More recent immigrants are usually the products of rapid Third World urbanization. Those from cities are often quite Westernized and accustomed to living a lifestyle similar to typical Americans. Urbanized persons will often be more open in their thinking regarding life and the world; some may even be quite secular. Rural persons, however, tend to adhere more faithfully to folk Islam, the syncretistic blending of classical Islam with indigenous pagan customs.

3. Interest Muslims in your holy and holistic Christian lifestyle.

In contextualizing the messenger, our primary goals should be to arouse curiosity concerning a devout, radically Christian lifestyle which is logical, natural, highly moral, practical, holistic and equitable; and to disprove Muslim stereotypes regarding Christian spirituality and morality.

Muslims almost always approach Christians with an attitude of superiority. The adherents of Islam are convinced that their faith is more logical (no "irrational" concepts such as the Trinity), more natural (all men and women are born Muslims), less contradictory (allegedly not so many different divisions and sects), more moral (Muslims still adhere strongly to a concept of Law), more holistic (it provides a "package" approach to life and culture), more practical (it provides more specific directions for everyday life) and more equitable (it equates men and women and all races and ethnic groups) than Christianity. As ministers of the gospel, we must correct these misconceptions and try to erase this attitude of superiority.

In dealing with these claims apologetically, some general issues need to be discussed. First, apologetics is essentially *defensive* in its orientation; the word *apologia* itself means "a defense." Apologetics are best used when someone has taken the offensive against us. Perhaps the main usage of apologetic arguments is to show that one has considered the objections made to one's religious beliefs and taken time to seek answers. Such arguments will seldom move a Muslim closer to the kingdom of God, but sincere answers may help to convince the Muslim opponent of the Christian's sincerity and devoutness.

Immigrants from Muslim countries come from a culture in which heated debate is considered one of the spices of life. Many Muslims tend to become emotional in the midst of what they consider to be a good argument, and such a display can be quite intimidating to more soft-spoken Westerners. A Muslim who senses that a Christian opponent is succumbing will often become louder and more insistent in trying to conclude and win the debate. For most American Christians, it takes some time to get used to discussions with Muslims. What we consider to be heated discussions Muslims view as normal conversations.

Deal only with the questions that arise. Do not bring up other areas of possible controversy which might not be issues for this particular Muslim.

Your goal in a defense of Christianity should be to show that your Christian walk is the equal of any Muslim's religious life. It may be shown to be superior, since the Muslim approach to matters of faith is essentially external and institutional, while yours is internal and personal *as well as* external and institutional.

4. Give Muslims day-to-day contact.

Some of the most significant reasons why Muslims do not convert to Christianity are sociological rather than theological, and personal contact with Christians on a day-to-day basis is what Muslims need. Muslims often refuse to become Christians not because they are convinced of Christianity's errors but for quite different reasons. They see no reason to change. They have been taught that Islam is better than Christianity—though often they do not have a clear idea of *why*.

How Christianity exceeds Islam

Muslims have never been confronted with claims that the Bible's teachings are superior to Muhammad's—and here is where Christians must take the offensive. Rather than dwelling on defensive apologetics, Christians should learn to highlight how Christianity most significantly exceeds the teachings of Islam. Following are the most essential:

1. *Conversion to Christianity produces an actual internal and personal change: a whole aspect of the human person—one's spirit—is "born again."* One becomes for the first time a complete person, with

body, soul and spirit intact and functioning. Such a change does not take place upon conversion to any other religion, including Islam (John 3:1-6).

2. *Conversion to Christianity is accompanied by the indwelling of the Holy Spirit in each believer.* This Spirit—who is "God with and in us"—empowers and enables us to live the life which God wants us to live (John 14:26; 16:8-13). No other faith, including Islam, has this aspect of empowerment.

3. *Salvation in Christianity is provided not on the basis of good works but as a free gift from a loving God.* Salvation does not have to be earned and may be acquired at any time (Ephesians 2:8-9; Romans 3:28). This fact relieves us from the enormous burden of trying to please the Creator who will reward us for "righteous" living. The good news of Christianity is that God has provided for individual salvation in and through Jesus Christ, and acknowledgment of Jesus as Master of one's life is sufficient to gain it.

4. *The Christian can be assured of his eternal salvation even before the final judgment.* Jesus stated that His "sheep" could never be snatched from His hand (John 10:28). The Apostle John made it clear that those who believe in Christ already have eternal life (3:36). And the Apostle Paul taught that those in Christ will never be condemned (Romans 8:1). Muslims do not have this kind of assurance, for they cannot know before Judgment Day itself whether or not their good deeds are sufficient to allow them entry into Paradise.

Christianity, of course, has many other advantages over Islam, but these are the four most significant. For any one of these reasons, and certainly for the four combined, a Muslim could see that conversion to Christianity is highly beneficial.

Few Muslims have ever seen members of their community convert to Christianity, and so they have no sense of what this would be like. In Egypt, Lebanon and Palestine, sizable groups of Christians have maintained separate communities throughout the centuries since the Muslim conquests. But these are not *converts* to Christianity, and in many cases they do not present an attractive picture. Without seeing or hearing fellow Muslims who have been born again, they have no models to follow. And the fact that converts nearly always experience social ostracism complicates the situation enormously. As far as most Muslims are concerned, the disadvantages of converting to Christianity far outweigh any benefits.

Lack of role models

The lack of identifiable models will continue until some courageous individuals are willing to publicly profess their commitment to Christ. The initial converts in any given community will most likely be extraordinary people who are willing to endure the social consequences of changing their religious allegiance. But what about the comparatively large number of Christians in America already? Is it not possible for them to serve as models for new converts? Much depends upon the day-to-day experiences Muslims have with persons who call themselves Christians, for some who wear the name are not worthy of it. The born-again evangelical must be prepared to discuss "nominal Christians" and "biblically ignorant or disobedient" Christians.

Most Muslims think in terms of Roman Catholicism or Eastern Orthodoxy when they think of Christianity. Protestantism in general is an enigma to them, and evangelical Protestants are often a complete mystery. I have occasionally found it necessary to *insist* that I am a Christian after explaining that I do not admit the validity of a priesthood, do not believe that the communion elements are magically transformed into the body and blood of Christ, do not believe that Mary the mother of Jesus was sinless or that she can act as a mediator between God and human beings and so on.

Muslims have identified these beliefs with Christianity because of their historical encounters with people who hold these beliefs. Protestantism can be confusing for a Muslim, but it can also open doors to very significant discussions. In explaining differences between the divisions of Christianity, the Christian may be able to explore the Bible in-depth with a Muslim friend.

But when all is said and done, the evangelical's lifestyle buys him a hearing—or closes the door to further contact. Muslims have expectations of how truly religious persons live their everyday lives, and unless Christians meet these standards, Muslims will not usually listen. The Christian's goal must be not only to meet the standard but to exceed it in ways that will make Muslims curious about the quality of life that the truly biblical Christian leads.

Notes

1   I use the word "relative" intentionally, since scholars disagree as to the actual conditions for Christians and Jews living under Islamic suzerainty during the Middle Ages. Some claim that, with exceptions, Christians and Jews were fairly well treated, and conversions to the Muslim faith were strictly voluntary. Others, however, insist that all non-Muslims suffered brutal treatment—including confiscation of homes and material possessions, rape and enslavement—throughout the centuries. For an in-depth treatment of this subject, see Bat Ye'or, *The Decline of Eastern Christianity under Islam* (Teaneck, NJ: Fairleigh Dickinson University Press, 1996).

2   There were, of course, exceptions. The Roman Catholic Ignatius of Loyola (1493-1559) founded the Society of Jesus (popularly known as the Jesuits) partly as a missionary order to reach Muslims for Christ. All early Jesuits were required to learn Arabic for this purpose.

3   See such passages as Deuteronomy 7:16: "You must destroy all the peoples the LORD your God gives over to you. Do not look on them with pity and do not serve their gods, for that will be a snare to you."

4   See George Otis, Jr., *The Last of the Giants: Lifting the Veil on Islam and the End Times* (Grand Rapids, MI: Chosen Books, 1991).

11

Evangelizing "Don'ts"

In the previous chapter we looked at relating to Muslims at the basic level of humanity. In this chapter we will look at some of the inevitable conflicts that arise when persons of different cultures and religious backgrounds form personal relationships and how we can avoid or counter them.

Be Careful When Dealing with ...

The potential for offending Muslims is great, so we will consider some of the chief areas of concern.

Food

Americans are casual toward the kinds of food we eat and toward mealtimes in general. For most of the world, food is a serious proposition. Meals are to be enjoyed and lingered over; they are important parts of a day's routine. Mealtime is for socializing; eating alone is an alien concept to many—perhaps most—of the world's people. And while fast-food chains are invading nearly every major city of the world, the idea of a "fast meal" is only slowly catching on.

Even more important is that Muslims will not eat food products prohibited by their scriptures, such as anything originating from the pig (pork, bacon, lard, shortening, etc.). Orthodox Muslims will not eat food that is not prepared according to Muslim law. These items are designated as *halal*, which means the same as kosher. If you invite Muslims to your home for a meal, or even for coffee and dessert, some may refuse to come. They fear that you will offer food that they cannot lawfully eat and they will feel embarrassed to refuse. You can assure them that you will provide foods that will not violate their convictions. If you live in a large city, suggest dinner at a Middle Eastern restaurant that advertises its menu as *halal*.

Clothing

In most of the world, clothes are not as important or as abundant as in America. The world's poorer peoples—including many Muslim groups—own only a single outfit or two and do not understand why Westerners need so many garments. They choose clothing for functionality and comfort, not for style or appearance. For many Muslims, clothing is important as a means of preserving a strict moral ethic. Some groups allow females to expose only their eyes and hands to the outside world. Few are this extreme, but one should generally expect Muslims to be secretly or openly offended by what most Americans wear.

This is particularly true of women; anything that reveals or accentuates the female figure can be a stumbling block. Immodest dress will embarrass adults and can be a temptation for young males in particular. Whereas in America the female breast may be considered the chief sex symbol, this is not necessarily so in other cultures. A woman's long flowing hair, legs, ankles, eyes and lips are in many cases the chief "turn-ons" for Muslim males.

At this point we should deal with a question that nearly always arises. How much should we change our lifestyles to avoid offending people? The Apostle Paul gave his personal philosophy regarding this question in First Corinthians 9:22 where he states that his desire was to become all things to all people in order to win them to Christ. But what about the fact that adaptations made in order to relate more effectively to one group may be offensive to another group? There is no simple answer.

Perhaps the wisest policy is to find a simple lifestyle that allows one to avoid giving offense. Ecclesiastes 7:16-18 offers some excellent guidelines when the writer advises us to be neither over-righteous nor over-wicked. Heeding this counsel will allow individuals to maintain their convictions on clothing and the like, while imitating the Apostle Paul's strategy of "becoming all things to all men" (see 1 Corinthians 9:22) Applying this principle to clothing, a Christian should acquire a tasteful yet simple wardrobe which is modest without being extreme.

Morality

Because of their commitment to following the Qur'an, most adherents of Islam are morally conservative compared to typical Americans, even American Christians. The majority of Muslims have high ethical standards and experience difficulty with the "looseness" of American society. This is particularly true in sexuality; among Muslims, females and (theoretically) males are expected to maintain their virginity until marriage.

This fact has significant social repercussions. Few Muslims approve of the American dating system; to believe that a male and female can be alone together without succumbing to their desire for sexual intercourse is considered appallingly naive. Within some communities young people are allowed to meet only in adult-chaperoned groups. Many Muslim parents are experiencing the problems of maintaining such a strict policy with their children, most of whom watch television, attend public schools and are exposed to a different ethic than their parents were as young people. Because Christian parents do not generally appear to find fault with dating, their spirituality becomes suspect.

These high standards apply in other areas as well. *Family* is very important to Muslims; they stick together and stand up for each other. Family honor is held in high regard; one must never shame one's family. Here things can get slippery from a Christian point of view, for some Middle Easterners will occasionally lie or withhold part of the truth to preserve family honor. In many religions—including Islam—certain kinds of lies do not carry the stigma that they do in Christianity.

Christians find it difficult to discern between a "malicious lie," one that is intended to deceive, and a "polite lie," one which intends to avoid giving offense. Most Muslims will bend over backward not to offend a host or hostess. They will sometimes say what they believe a person wants to hear or say things which are not technically true in order not to impose, and this is perfectly acceptable within their worldview. While from the Christian standpoint it may seem contradictory that a Muslim would uphold high ethical standards and yet indulge in "polite lies," from a Muslim perspective this is not contradictory at all.

Another difficulty is the Muslim attitude regarding pets. It is impossible for some to imagine having a dog in one's house. A dog is seen as a farm animal, like a cow or goat, animals which we would never have in our homes. Do not be insulted if Muslims avoid your dog or treat it in an unfriendly manner. It may be best simply to confine pets to another room during a visit by adherents of Islam.

Gender issues

An enormous difference exists in how women are typically viewed and treated in America versus most of the rest of the world. This can be one of the most difficult issues that Christian females will face when dealing with the adherents of Islam. While the Qur'an in theory upholds a type of equality between men and women, this equality has either not been applied or has been interpreted differently by various Muslim

cultures. To say that women are subordinate or inferior in Islam is much too simplistic, but Christians
may become offended by the ways some Muslim
males treat their wives and daughters. But here we will
have to exercise a great amount of patience and a bit
of cultural self-reflection.

Just three or four generations ago, American society was much like many Muslim societies today.
The women's movements in America have made
enormous changes over the last several decades.
But it is important to remember that feminist views
are held almost exclusively by Americans and
Northern Europeans. It is definitely not advisable
to begin a private crusade to indoctrinate Muslims
with feminist teachings. One will make immediate
enemies of the males and, sometimes, the females
as well. This involves more than just sociological realities. Muslims believe their religious teachings
were revealed by God. To initiate radical changes
would, from an Islamic point of view, affront the
Deity Himself.

Closely related to this issue is the status of children. One can expect to see the reverse of what is
found in America, for here youth is worshiped and
old age is tucked away out of sight. Islam, on the
other hand, teaches that older persons are to be
venerated and that children are comparatively insig-
nificant until they reach a certain level of maturity.

In addition, discipline may appear much harsher
than that to which we are accustomed. In a culture
where almost any form of correction or discipline
can be interpreted as "child abuse," we will again
need to exercise patience and examine the basis of

our convictions. Christians will need to ask whether or not their beliefs have been shaped more by culture than by the Bible itself. They must be willing to admit that interaction with Muslims might actually point to a more "biblical" way of thinking than contemporary American Christianity does.

Stereotypes of Americans

The attitude that many Muslims in the world hold toward Americans can be summed up in two words: *resentment* and *antagonism*. They perceive America as a "world bully" that is always trying to force its own values—and products—upon other peoples of the world. Americans are considered loud, rude, arrogant, demanding, spoiled, pushy and just generally obnoxious.

In certain Muslim countries the feelings are even more extreme, such as in Iran during the revolution brought about by the Ayatollah Khomeini. The U.S., considered to be the bastion of secularism, materialism and immorality, was labeled "The Great Satan." Such an extreme attitude is rarely seen among immigrants, but occasionally one meets a Muslim who had only America to which to flee, and strong suspicions may remain. Usually a little down-home hospitality, friendliness, genuine care and a servant heart dispel these stereotypes.

On the other hand, some Muslims—particularly young people—view America with vastly different feelings: fascination, admiration and even adoration. America is Shangri-la, the Promised Land and never-never land all rolled into one. Some Christians have capitalized on this attitude by claiming that America and Europe are what they are because of the Christian faith. There is doubtless some truth to this idea. But one could just as easily make the case that America's *negative* aspects (from the Muslim's viewpoint) have resulted from Christianity as well. These include the "once-saved, always-saved" mentality, which many believe gives license to immorality, and the "health and wealth" gospel, which leads to materialism. This reasoning can work both ways.

Be Careful to Do ...

Before Christians can communicate the gospel effectively to Muslims, they must earn the right to be heard. They must work to establish credibility in accordance with First Thessalonians 4:11-12, where Paul counsels that Christians work with their hands. Paul states here that we must "win the respect of outsiders"; this means that we as Christians must live among Muslims and show a consistent Christian lifestyle.

Thus it becomes essential that Christians maintain the following disciplines in order to gain credibility with Muslims:

- Time spent daily in prayer, preferably more than once per day.

- Time spent daily in Bible study.

- Scripture memorization, by which is meant an ability to quote from memory a substantial number of verses.

- Fasting—for significant periods of time.

- Regular financial giving.

- Commitment to a conservative moral ethic, including opposition to abortion, feminism, homosexuality, premarital sexual intercourse, etc.

- Commitment to family values and to a "wholesome" family life.

Christians must talk and act as disciples of Jesus, and they must do so naturally, without effort or strain. They must live openly, boldly, joyously, simply, honestly, humbly and helpfully. But while we are gentle and kind, we must at the same time be clear. In simple, natural ways—talking about our faith as naturally as we would talk about sports or hobbies—we must make sure that Muslims understand why we are the way we are. Ultimately they must understand that our biblical faith is not what they have been taught that it is, but it nevertheless differs fundamentally from Islam.

Contextualizing the Christian Message for Muslims

In the previous chapter we talked about the importance of fitting *ourselves* for ministering to Muslims. Now, how must we prepare our *message*?

1. Know the points of contention.

Be aware of the major points of contention between Christians and Muslims and seek to prevent these from becoming immediate stumbling blocks at the beginning of an encounter. One can delineate three major areas of disagreement between Christians and Muslims.

- Theological contentions, which deal with the deity of Christ, the doctrine of the Trinity, the crucifixion and resurrection of Christ, the necessity of the substitutionary atonement and the trustworthiness and inerrancy of the Bible vis-a-vis the Qur'an.

- Practical contentions, which deal with the perceived lack of discipline of Christians regarding Bible study, Scripture memorization, consistency in prayer and fasting; the perceived immorality of the typical Christian, the "looseness" of Christians with regard to dietary principles, and, in certain contexts, the hypocrisy of Christians regarding the institution of polygamy.

- Historical contentions, which deal with the "crusader" or evangelical missionary attitude of Christians and/or Westerners in general, the syncretistic and materialistic trappings of Catholicism and Eastern Orthodoxy, and the stereotyping by Christians of Muslims as terrorists, etc.

2. Know the "common" ground.

Christians should also be able to acknowledge and discuss intelligently the aspects of theology that Muslims and Christians appear to have in common. Although ultimately there are no true points of contact between them, we may begin discussions with beliefs we *appear* to have in common.

Scriptural authority

Muslims, Jews and Christians together constitute the *ahl al-kitab* ("the people of the book"). The Qur'an specifically mentions the *tawrah* (Torah), or books of Moses and the rest of the Old Testament, and the *injil* (the Gospels), meaning the entire New Testament, as having been originally revealed by Allah. Muslims believe that both were corrupted, necessitating the revelation of the Qur'an to Muhammad, but the fact that Christians are committed to a holy book can serve as a starting point for discussion.

Patriarchs and prophets

Muslims and Christians alike venerate a number of the same Old Testament figures and prophets: Adam, Abraham, Isaac, Jacob, Moses, David, Isaiah and Jesus, to name but a few.

Jesus

Muslims venerate Jesus as a prophet of Allah and He is acknowledged in the Qur'an to be the Messiah. Muslims also speak of His virgin birth, His ability to perform miracles and His second coming.

Supernaturalistic worldview

Muslims believe, just as Christians do, that there is an unseen world around us, populated by angels and demons.

Mystical and supernatural experiences

Some Muslims give a great deal of credence to visions and dreams as well as certain kinds of miracles.

3. Realize you don't fit the stereotype.

A Christian who lives as a consistent Protestant will be a puzzle to many Muslims. Protestants—particularly evangelicals—are often surprised to learn that the majority of the world's Muslims see Christianity in terms of Roman Catholicism and Eastern Orthodoxy. Few have met or dealt with an evangelical Protestant. They view Christianity as an external and institutional phenomenon, with emphasis on the material splendor of the papacy and Vatican City, the gaudiness of the tourist sites in Israel and the like. Because of their lack of visibility and minority status, the credibility of Protestants is low; it is necessary for evangelicals to establish the biblical basis for their brand of Christianity.

4. Present your faith positively.

Concentrate on presenting New Testament faith positively rather than presenting Islam negatively. The fastest way to confirm Muslims in their faith is to challenge them directly. Even if they have been quite nominal in their everyday beliefs and practices, the moment a Christian challenges them, they become immediately and radically Muslim. As far as possible, keep dialogues low-key and build up the Christian faith rather than tearing down Islam.

5. Share faith experiences from both sides.

Concentrate on sharing personal experiences of faith from both sides, without presuppositions regarding what "typical Muslims" believe. Islam is a highly individual faith. Do not assume that you know what specific individuals believe; they will nearly always surprise you. And do not tell Muslims what you have been taught that they believe, for you may end up teaching them aspects of their faith of which they were unaware. Whatever one says concerning Muslim doctrine will usually be interpreted negatively, since it comes from an American, a Westerner, a Christian. Muslims will hasten to correct a Christian's statements, even if what was said actually fairly represented what they believe.

Be Careful to Use ...

A great deal of creativity is necessary to communicate the gospel message to Muslims. A variety of approaches are available, but contemporary evangelists are often not as well-versed in certain forms as they need to be. The following methods are arranged in an order that shows increasing distance between the communicator and the recipient. Ideally one should attempt to use the method with the most personal contact, moving down the scale only when a specific social or political situation necessitates increased distance.

Storytelling

Storytelling, as opposed to propositional teaching techniques, is an art which involves weaving the gospel message into vignettes similar to Jesus' parables. Narratives are easily dramatized, although such techniques are generally unfamiliar to most Western Christian workers. The style of writing which characterizes Max Lucado's books would be a useful place to begin.

Christians will need to learn to portray biblical figures and their teachings in this manner for the Muslim context. Christian evangelists will want to emphasize stories about their lives and spiritual experiences as well, allowing Muslims to share life experiences in return. In constructing a narrative of one's conversion experience, Acts 26 is an excellent model, for here the apostle Paul tells the story of his own spiritual journey, complete with elementary doctrinal truths at the end.

The Gospels and Acts are written in narrative fashion and are of paramount importance in Muslim work. For many Christians, however, the New Testament will need to be reread and in some cases reinterpreted from an experiential rather than didactic point of view. For instance, instead of approaching the letters of First and Second Corinthians from the standpoint of "principles regarding conduct in the institutional church," one may speak of them in this way: "Paul the apostle was living in the city of Ephesus during a two-and-a-half year period on his third missionary journey. He wrote to the followers of Jesus who lived in Corinth concerning some of the difficulties they were experiencing living godly lives in the midst of an ungodly world."

Here are several points with which Muslims can identify: apostleship (Muhammad was a *rasul,* an apostle); city living (Islam has always been a religion of the cities); missionary expansion (*da'wah* in Islam); and godly living in an ungodly world (a perennial problem for spiritually minded persons).

Dialogue

While storytelling usually takes place in relaxed and informal settings such as individual homes, exchanges between Christians and Muslims of a more formal nature have been taking place for many years, particularly within ecumenical circles. There are, however, different kinds of dialogues. Some seek only to gain information concerning an alternative religious community while others have more directly evangelistic purposes. The motivation prompting such encounters will determine how effective (or ineffective) they are in eliciting conversions. Obviously, for evangelical Christians a mere exchange of information will not fulfill the biblical mandate for communicating the gospel to all creation.

Debates

In recent years, debates have become a popular avenue for bringing together Christians and Muslims in the hope that the gospel message might be presented during the exchange. Encounters have been arranged between various well-known Christians and such contemporary Muslim apologists as Ahmed Deedat, undoubtedly the most famous Muslim debater. Josh McDowell, John Gilchrist, Anis Shorrosh, Jimmy Swaggart and other Christians have debated Deedat publicly, as well as several lesser-known personages.

Unfortunately, Deedat and other representatives of his Islamic Propagation Centre usually come out ahead. Evidentialist apologetics has historically had very little value in winning Muslims to Christ. Such an approach favors an externally and institutionally oriented religion such as Islam, and the temperament of Muslims conforms more readily to debate than does that of most Christians.

Preaching campaigns

In few places in today's world can open-air preaching of the gospel to Muslims take place. But in some countries where Muslims are a minority or where an officially secular government maintains religious pluralism, possibilities exist for such campaigns. The Billy Graham Evangelistic Association, for instance, employs Muslim evangelist Abdiyah Akbar Abdul-Haqq, who writes of opportunities he has had to preach the gospel before Muslim audiences in India in *Sharing Your Faith with a Muslim*.

Radio outreach

This method broadcasts the gospel and basic Bible studies throughout the Middle East and North Africa. Correspondence course materials can be ordered free of charge. Several mission agencies have used TransWorld Radio's facilities and have developed programs in Arabic, Urdu and other languages and dialects spoken by Muslims in this part of the world.

Some organizations have reported success using this method because materials can be ordered anonymously through the mail service. This avoids the social pressures and ostracism which would arise if a person publicly exhibited interest in Christianity. Without personal contact, however, it is nearly impossible to ascertain how many persons make a profession of faith or to gather into churches those who do.

Discipleship for Converts
from Islam to Christianity

When Muslims become Christians, they are often cast out of their homes, disinherited, fired from their jobs and subjected to social ostracism and even persecution. They lose the all-encompassing network of family and community. Their need for a substitute family and companions must be supplied by the body of Christ, or the multitude of changes affecting their lives may overwhelm them.

Therefore, whenever and wherever possible, we need to work with Muslims as groups, as families when various members come to Christ simultaneously, or as gatherings of individuals in other circumstances. In his work among Muslims in Bangladesh, Phil Parshall encouraged converts to postpone baptism until a significant number could undergo this ordinance at the same time, forming the nucleus of a new church. This provides a support group for all who choose to leave Islam for the Christian faith.

The discipling of Muslim converts will in most cases need to be conducted with an Eastern rather than a Western philosophy of education. Western educational philosophy is based on an Aristotelian model involving a teacher and student, two persons who are essentially disconnected by a gap of professionalism. Eastern philosophy speaks in terms of a master who acts as a father figure and mentor to the disciple.

In Western thinking, the teacher's task is simply to transfer knowledge to the mind of the student. This knowledge (in theory) is sufficient to produce a desired behavior or attitude in the student's life. The teacher does not need to practice or experience what he teaches; indeed, the personal life of the teacher is irrelevant. He just needs the requisite knowledge of a subject and the ability to communicate that knowledge.

Eastern thinking is radically different; it never assumes that the mere transfer of knowledge is sufficient to produce a specific behavior or attitude. Rather, it believes that knowledge is useless without both a *model* illustrating how such knowledge may be applied and *motivation* to practically apply it. For this reason, the master *must* practice what he teaches; his personal life provides the model and often the motivation for the disciple to follow.

The master/disciple model plays an important role in providing the kind of close relationship necessary for the new Christian to be successfully grounded in the faith and to continue his growth toward maturity.

The Church for Converts
from Islam to Christianity

In recent years some have suggested that Christian missionary agents should seek to establish "Jesus mosques," institutions designed for converts from Islam using the philosophy that has produced

"Messianic fellowships" for converts from Judaism. Some proponents of this idea even say that Islam should be treated more as a Christian heresy than as a competing world religion. They say that Islam is really quite close to the Christian faith, requiring only a few small alterations to bring Muslims within the bounds of orthodox Christianity. Few, however, advocate this approach. The chief criticism is that it fails to clarify the significant distinctions between Islam and Christianity and opens the door to, at best, confusion and, at worst, syncretism.[1]

A more favored approach to the concept of church planting among Muslims is a return to the fundamental elements as seen in the book of Acts, First Corinthians 12:4-31; 14:26-40 and the books of First and Second Timothy. The examples and principles in these passages present the essence of the New Testament Church without the accretions of nearly 2,000 years of church history. Transference of core ecclesiastical concepts into an Islamic culture is infinitely easier than transference of a fully developed Western model, such as those found in American denominations. In *New Paths in Muslim Evangelism*, Phil Parshall gives several suggestions for such a Muslim-convert church.[2]

In Western countries, where Muslims form only a tiny minority within large populations, converts can more easily assimilate into traditional church structures. Muslim families and communities in the West do not enforce the same kinds of social constraints as in solidly Muslim countries.

But even in America, it is important to surround Muslim converts with open-hearted, hospitable and service-oriented Christian brothers and sisters. Our Christian fellowships must provide the same kinds of support and networking opportunities that Muslims enjoyed in their Islamic communities. If we fail at this task, our young brothers and sisters in Christ may not be able to endure the loneliness of their new circumstances, and they may be drawn into Christian cults or back into Islam. Such an end would be tragic beyond description.

Notes

1   See Greg Livingstone, *Planting Churches in Muslim Cities: A Team Approach* (Grand Rapids, MI: Baker Book House, 1993), 179. See also the following articles for recent discussions of this issue: Erich Bridges, "Of 'Jesus Mosques' and Muslim Christians," *Mission Frontiers Bulletin*, July-October 1997, 19-21; and Don Eenigenburg, "The Pros and Cons of Islamicized Contextualization," *Evangelical Missions Quarterly*, July 1997, 310-315.
2   See Phil Parshall, *New Paths in Muslim Evangelism* (Grand Rapids, MI: Baker Book House, 1980), 157-180.

12

Reaching African-
American Muslims

Carl F. Ellis, Jr.

A s we have already pointed out, the majority of
African-American Muslims are "mainline"
Muslims. They tend to view the Black nationalist
Muslims as not genuinely Islamic. Among this lat-
ter group, the most vocal and visible is the Nation of
Islam, headed by Louis Farrakhan. Remember,
however, this is only one of at least six groups calling
themselves "Nation of Islam."

Why Muslims Choose Islam

When approaching a Muslim in any of these
sects, it is helpful to evaluate why the person has

embraced Islam. Three considerations are important.

First, he could be attracted by the standards of Islam—the doctrine, theology and teaching. Most Christians seem to assume that this is why a person embraces any belief system. However, two other considerations are more important in understanding a person's reasons for becoming a Muslim.

Second, the person could be attracted to Islam because of his situation—feelings of cultural displacement or alienation, social disorganization in "the 'hood," etc. This is especially true for the African-American underclass, who feel isolated from mainstream America and trapped in the ghetto. The individual often perceives brotherhood, cultural affirmation, solidarity and a regimen of discipline in the Muslim community, all of which counteract the effects of oppression.

To make matters worse, some well-meaning Christians who try to reach out to Muslims have inadvertently driven them further away with pictures of an effeminate, blond-haired, blue-eyed Jesus. This not only violates Muslim teachings concerning idolatry but also presents a Jesus who reinforces the underlying belief that Christianity is for Whites, while Islam is for Blacks.

Third, the person could be attracted to Islam because of his own motivations and goals—such as a desire for righteousness. Many people realize that they have been taken in by unattainable illusions of the "American dream." Others may want to purge themselves of false values. When they witness the

Islamic community with its disciplined, rigorous approach to life, they may see this as a means of satisfying their desire for righteousness. And some may realize that they have been alienated from God and desire to achieve His favor.

"Jesus-ianity"

One of the great mistakes we tend to make in approaching Muslims is forcing a "Jesus-ianity" concept—getting to "the point" of the message too quickly. I have often heard Christians tell Muslims, "Well, Jesus is God." And certainly He is God. But how did Jesus Himself reveal His deity? The Lord found creative and effective ways to communicate the truth without directly saying it. Observe, for example, how Jesus revealed His identity to the disciples on the road to Emmaus (Luke 24:13-35).

To say "Jesus is God" will sound to a Muslim as if we are deifying a mere man. But from a biblical perspective, we know that the second Person in the Godhead became a man in Jesus Christ. This is *incarnation*, not deification. This distinction is seldom communicated to Muslims. It is imperative, however, that they understand that God alone is the object of our worship and that God's decision to become a man in no way diminished His deity.

How to Reach Out

Instead of simply confronting a Muslim by pitting my doctrine against his, I seek to draw him out through conversation. I meet many Muslims whose personal goals and motivations are essentially biblical. In such cases, I have learned to be sympathetic and supportive. Others I encounter have a passion for community development. Not only do I disclose how I share this passion, I also point out how the Bible speaks to this concern.

One example is Nehemiah. Here was a young minority "brother" who found great success as a highly paid professional in the Persian government. From the text it is obvious that his powerful position in the king's palace (the Persian "White House") was not merely the result of "affirmative action." Yet he put his career on the line and used the considerable resources at his disposal to empower and advance his people back in Jerusalem ("the 'hood"). As a result of sharing such insights from the Bible, barriers have fallen.

Only after establishing such camaraderie will a discussion concerning the means of achieving their goals become meaningful. Then the gospel literally becomes "good news." The discussion can take several directions. In brief, the following dialogue illustrates my three basic approaches.

Righteousness approach

Carl: "Isn't God perfectly righteous?"

Muslim: "Yes, of course."

Carl: "Is it true that God tolerates no unrighteousness whatsoever?"

Muslim: "Yes."

Carl: "Isn't God perfectly just?"

Muslim: "Yes."

Carl: "Doesn't God's perfect justice mean that He will punish all unrighteousness?"

Muslim: "Certainly."

Carl (this is where I gently lower the boom): "Are you perfectly righteous?"

Muslim: "No! And nobody is."

Carl: "Since God tolerates no unrighteousness, then God cannot tolerate you."

Muslim: "Yes, but I'm striving for righteousness."

Carl: "But that doesn't change the fact that God doesn't tolerate you because of unrighteousness. It also doesn't change the fact that because God is just, you must also be punished for your unrighteousness up to now."

A Muslim has no real solution to this dilemma. The best answer he can offer is that God forgives by simply saying, "I forgive." But the Muslim still lacks assurance of this forgiveness.

Muslim: "If I can't approach God, then you can't either."

Carl: "Oh yes, I can, and I do."

Muslim: "How?"

Carl: "I come to God on the basis of the perfect righteousness of Jesus Christ."

I then share that God's forgiveness comes through justification in Christ alone and that I can have assurance of it. A Muslim cannot deny the perfect righteousness of Christ because the Qur'an states it clearly (see Suras 3:40-41 and 19:9). An explanation of justification now begins to make sense.

Relationship approach

Carl: "How would you describe your relationship with God?"

Muslim: "I'm a servant of God, responsible to submit to His will."

Carl: "Would you also describe yourself as a slave of God?"

Muslim: "Yes, this is what the Qur'an teaches."

Carl: "This is interesting, because I am a *son* of God."

If my Muslim friend knows his doctrine well, this statement might be repulsive to him. To prevent this response, I explain that my sonship is based on *adoption*. I then introduce the teachings of Hebrews 3:1-6, comparing Moses, the servant of God, to Christ, the Son of God. I explain that Christian sonship is greater than Islamic servanthood because the son, not the servant, is honored in the Father's house.

Submission approach

During a stimulating discussion I once had with a Muslim, he concluded by saying, "Carl, you're a Muslim, and you don't know it."

"That's not true," I replied. "I know I'm a Muslim." My response caught him completely off guard.

In Arabic, the term *Muslim* means "one who submits," generally understood to mean "one who submits to the will of God." The term *Islam* means "submission," or in its popular understanding, "submission to the will of God."

As a disciple of Jesus Christ, I am in submission to the will of God. This makes me a true "Muslim." At this point, I usually share Romans 10:1-4. Although this passage refers to non-believing Jews who have "a zeal for God, but not according to knowledge" (see Romans 10:2, KJV), it could also apply to Muslims. Muslims, like first-century Jews, live under a law of discipline. According to the Bible, however, true Islam is *submission* to God's way of putting people right, and that way is Jesus Christ.

Just as I am a true son of Abraham by the power of Jesus Christ, I can also be considered a true Muslim by the same power. At this point, I sometimes refer back to my "righteousness approach."

A word of caution: This "submission approach" must be used carefully and sparingly. It is most effective when the Muslim introduces it as in the above dialogue. It is not wise to take the initiative and claim to be a Muslim. This will lead to counter-productive arguments about doctrines and definitions.

Patience

The Islamic community is in many respects equivalent to the Jewish community in the first century. Our approach to Muslims must therefore be similar to the apostle Paul's approach to his Jewish brothers. In acknowledging that non-believing Jews have a zeal for God, Paul has given us a biblical example of his approach. This "zeal," he says, is not according to true knowledge. In essence, he is saying, "Though they have the right goals and motivations, they have adopted the wrong means for achieving those goals and satisfying those motivations."

I have talked to dozens of Muslims who, in the final analysis, have admitted they can do nothing to earn God's favor—nothing to save themselves. Their only hope of salvation is God. Such a belief is even consistent with the Qur'an (Sura 6:70). Is not this the essence of the gospel of our Lord Jesus Christ?

God promises His Word will not return void (see Isaiah 55:11, KJV), and if through a skillful communication of God's Word, a Muslim begins to understand the truths of the gospel, God will surely honor it. If we simply plant the seed and water it, God will "give the increase" (see 1 Corinthians 3:7, KJV). However, we often find ourselves oriented toward "instant salvations" and "instant decisions"—just add a few spiritual laws, we say. But it does not work that way with Muslims. They need time, patience and, most of all, love. Meanwhile, God is faithful.

Power

As I taught a seminar in a Midwestern prison, an inmate named Ahmad spoke with me several times. Only toward the end of the seminar did I begin to understand why. He seemed to be saying, "Brother Carl, I may be a Muslim, but I'm hurting. When I get out of this place, I don't know if I can stay out of crime. Do you have anything to offer me? What is this power you keep talking about? I pray five times a day. I don't eat pork. I keep all the Muslim disciplines. But I just don't seem to have this power. How can I get it?"

I began to share with Ahmad that subscribing to all these disciplinary procedures—trying to earn God's favor—was futile. I told him that the Qur'an's earlier verses actually endorse the teachings of the Bible. Early Muslims were commanded in the Qur'an to respect what the Bible says (Suras 5:50-51; 6:92; 10:37-38, 94; 35:40).[1] And what does the Bible say about human attempts to please God by means of "good deeds"? According to Isaiah 64:6, "all our righteous acts are like filthy rags."

I told Ahmad that if he would receive God's gift of grace through Jesus Christ and subscribe to a life of discipline as a means of expressing his faith and thanksgiving to God, then he would be in balance. And having received God's grace through Christ, he would also receive God's power to stay out of crime.

Resonance

Omar is a close friend from the South who, like me, was profoundly affected by the great struggle of African-Americans during the 1960s and beyond. When we first met, a special bond quickly developed between us and has continued to this day. We have had many discussions about the canonization of Scripture and the nature of Jesus. Eventually he admitted that Jesus is more than a prophet.

Like Omar, many Muslims I meet grew up in the church. These persons have a veneer of Islam, but *intuitively* they have what is essentially a Christian outlook. It is important to remember that historically, African-American theology has always been more intuitive than rational. Therefore, if we learn to deal with a Muslim skillfully on a rational basis, God's Word will resonate with that intuitive Christian core. This will affect him in more ways than he is willing to admit. This is in keeping with what the prophet Isaiah stated:

> As the rain and the snow
>   come down from heaven,
> and do not return to it
>   without watering the earth
> and making it bud and flourish,
>   so that it yields seed for the sower and
>   bread for the eater,
> so is my word that goes out from my mouth:
>   It will not return to me empty,
> but will accomplish what I desire
>   and achieve the purpose for which I sent it.
>   (55:10-11)

Adaptability

On the day of Pentecost, by the power of the Holy Spirit, the gospel of Jesus Christ was preached and applied in many languages to many cultures. The gospel is unique in that it is culturally adaptable in any situation without losing its integrity.[2] Anyone can come to Christ, regardless of his culture or language. Unfortunately, the way we practice Christianity today is inconsistent with the cultural flexibility seen in the Bible. We too often give the impression that our gospel is inextricably tied to the dominant American culture.

In Islam, on the other hand, no language or culture other than Arabic is tolerated in spiritual matters. Thus, in worship and prayer, the non-Arabic culture and language of the Muslim must be left outside the door. It is therefore ironic that despite Islam's usual cultural intolerance, Muslims have done a better job than Christians in affirming African-American roots and culture.

It is not too late, however, for the Christian witness to make an impact. By learning how to apply Scripture to the situations, motivations and goals of those attracted to Islam, we can skillfully, lovingly and wisely communicate the gospel to Muslims. The response we get will not be instant, but it will be lasting.

Not only our words must be adapted to reach Muslims. Our lifestyles may need to be changed as well. For instance, I met Yusef in a city on the East Coast. He, like Omar, was raised in the church and had become a Muslim. However, through the reasoned and loving witness of a friend, he was led to Christ. I took him out to dinner where we had an intense discussion about reaching other Muslims.

As we ordered dinner I jokingly asked, "Hey, bro, are you back on the swine (pork) yet?" He laughed and said, "No, man, I keep the discipline for the sake of ministry to my Islamic brothers." Over dinner he explained how keeping his disciplined lifestyle and his Arabic name enabled him to make remarkable breakthroughs with Muslims. (Here we see echoes of Paul's personal testimony in First Corinthians 9:19-22.)

We also need flexibility in our approach to the concept of "church." If someone like Omar, for instance, comes to Christ, how will the churches respond to him? Will they be sensitive, or will they continue to be ill-equipped to deal with those who come to Christ from a Muslim background? As we begin to deal with Muslims more effectively, we will need to develop appropriate, alternative, "Muslim friendly" models of the church. We will also need new types of Christians who, like Yusef, will practice their faith in an Islamic lifestyle.

Practical Suggestions

If you sense God's calling to minister to African-American Muslims, here are some practical suggestions:

- Be yourself.

- Try to understand Islamic doctrine from the perspective of Islam. Recognize that Muhammad encountered a very corrupt form of Christianity. Study the history of Islam's development, especially among African-Americans.

- Be a good listener. Don't evaluate a Muslim only on the basis of his doctrine. Examine the situation that led him to Islam and the goals he is trying to achieve through it.

- When the motivation and goals of the Muslim are biblical, affirm them. When they are not, lovingly challenge them. And whenever possible, use words according to a Muslim's definitions, not yours.

- When dealing with a Muslim's doctrine, do not use the occasion to show him how much you know about his faith. Instead, deal with him on the basis of what he expresses to you about his beliefs. You will find that he is never totally consistent with the doctrine he holds.

- It is always important to draw out a Muslim by asking questions in a spirit genuinely wanting to be informed. Give him a chance to express himself and make sure he knows you understand what he is saying. Ask him, "Is this what you mean?" Then try to summarize his point(s). If he answers affirmatively, proceed to evaluate, critique or challenge.

- Consider the encounter to be similar to a tennis match. Allow your "opponent" to give you his best shot; then gently lob the ball back to his side of the court. Let him make the mistakes; then move in with your game plan. In other words, do not be bowled over by his arguments. Stand firm, with poise and confidence.

- Remember, just as there is superficial religion among professing Christians, there will be the same among professing Muslims. Things are not always what they seem. If you are familiar with Islamic theology, you can usually tell when a Muslim begins to feel the pinch. He may begin to repeat himself or make up his theology on the spot. When this happens, do not take advantage of his vulnerability by lording it over him. Rather, seek to communicate subtly but clearly that you are aware of his tenuous position. The very fact that you refuse to pulverize him will communicate more about the validity of the Christian faith than if you devastate him with your rational arguments.

- Do not use a King James Bible. According to the teachings of some Muslim sects, King James himself translated this version and corrupted it. I recommend the New International Version.

- Never use a Bible in which you have made marks. To a Muslim, this indicates a disrespect for the Word of God.

- Avoid all pictures of God, Jesus or any biblical characters, whether they be blue-eyed with blond hair or brown-eyed with Afros.

- Although in most cases the African-American Muslim community may be a de facto Black group, do not initiate discussions regarding issues of race. Many mainline Muslims have a humanistic slant and see themselves as having matured beyond an identity of Blackness. According to their humanistic claims, therefore, being Black or White should not pose barriers.

- Never use the word "Trinity." From Scripture, we know that God's oneness of being is never diminished by His Tri-personhood. But because of Islam's teaching, this word often connotes the worship of three gods and will bog a discussion down with issues of polytheism. There are many ways to express the Trinitarian concept. One way, for example, is to use the term "Godhead."

- Don't be offended by the Muslim's use of the term Allah—this is simply the Arabic word for "God."

- In dealing with Muslims, avoid anything that will give offense—except the cross.

- Finally, and most importantly, never forget the power of prayer and love. For against these there is no defense, Islamic or otherwise.

Notes

1 These early passages were recited in the hostile environment of Mecca. There, Muhammad reached out to Christians and Jews seeking friendships and alliances. The later quranic passages, recited in Medina, were harsh and militaristic—endorsing war and repressive measures toward non-Muslims. Muhammad ruled Medina with an iron fist.

 According to Islamic teaching, when passages contradict each other, the later passage cancels the earlier one. In the same way, quranic passages cancel conflicting biblical passages. This is called the Doctrine of Abrogation.

 In dialogue with Muslims, it is not wise to introduce this doctrine, for they may be unaware of it. However, if the Muslim seems to disregard your citation of biblical or early quranic passages, it is probably because of the Doctrine of Abrogation.

 Just remember that a correct and wise application of Scripture to core issues still has a power against which there is no defense.

2 See, for instance, Lamin Sanneh, *Translating the Message* (Maryknoll, NY: Orbis, 1989) for a description of the advantages which Christianity has over Islam due to the former's translatability.

Conclusion

What can we expect for the future of Islam in America? While whatever we say must be seen as somewhat tentative, I believe that we can safely predict some things.

First, the number of Muslims living in America will continue to grow slowly. This increase will partly come from immigration, for there is no sign that the social unrest in many Muslim lands will disappear in the foreseeable future.

Secularization (the process which dichotomizes one's religious life and the institutions of human life), *nationalism* (the issue of identification more by territorial or genetic background than by religious faith) and *fundamentalism* (an ideology which attempts to return a religious faith to its "pristine" condition, looking solely to scriptural and foundational sources for life choices) are deeply rooted in the Muslim world. Strife arising from these philosophies will continue to drive Muslims to lands where pluralistic democracy allows them to adopt—or reject—them without harm. More and more, "the huddled masses yearning to breathe free" will include the citizens of Muslim countries.

Growth through conversion will continue as well, albeit equally slow. Currently, conversion to Islam in America is still seen as essentially an African-American phenomenon. Thus such a change in religious allegiance is of little—if any—interest to White or Hispanic Americans. The few Whites who choose to become Muslims are categorized as odd, or in some other sense maladjusted individuals, who need the psychological "thrill" of an exotic, nontraditional religious faith.

This perception will gradually change as an increasing number of testimonies by Anglo-Muslims are highlighted in Muslim periodicals and as some of these converts begin to assume leadership roles in mosques and Islamic Centers. As more people like Jeffrey Lang and Jodi Anway publicize their conversions and experiences as members of the Muslim faith, other Anglos will find it easier to consider the possibility of changing their religious allegiance.[1] The momentum will eventually lead to a general social acceptance of conversion to Islam for others besides African-Americans.

What Will Islam Be Like?

Precisely what form Islam will take in America is still unclear. While we described the general profile of a convert in chapters 3 and 4, we said nothing of the two distinct groups which are now beginning to appear. One of these groups I would designate as "conservative," in the sense that adherents seek to conserve the form of the religion as they found it or as they have idealized it. Their conversion resulted because Islam is different from religious systems familiar in America, such as Christianity, Judaism and the New Age religions. These conservative converts are characterized by the following:

- An often overzealous enthusiasm for their new faith with a concomitant rejection of their former faith and, often, of family members and/or friends who insist upon remaining within the old paradigm.

- A largely naive, uncritical acceptance of all the beliefs and practices of their newly adopted religion.

- A tendency to follow these beliefs and practices consistently and to defend them fiercely, whether or not they are culturally acceptable or even conform to common sense within that culture.

- An evangelical zeal to introduce others to their newfound faith and to convince them of its validity.

But one wonders how enticing this form of Islam will actually be in the contemporary West. These converts preach radical opposition to both Christianity and Judaism. They advocate a theocratic form of government and in general are opposed to pluralistic democracy. Their rhetoric regarding Israel and its American support is inflammatory.

Their advocacy of traditional Islamic social practices and communal values would keep Muslims at the fringes of Western society, inviting suspicion and the continuation of inaccurate stereotypes. It seems clear that if this form of Islam were to become predominantly accepted and practiced in the West, relations between Muslims and non-Muslims would be tense and confrontational.

Adherents of a second group, which I call "liberal" converts, are in many ways the diametric opposite of the conservatives. They are characterized by the following:

- A lesser likelihood of abandoning completely their former faith, with a concomitant striving to maintain cordial relationships with friends and relatives.

- A tendency to analyze and examine critically their newly adopted faith, with a greater openness either to adapt or reject unsuitable aspects.

- Willingness to refine the beliefs and practices of their new faith, forging compromises or even syncretisms between the former belief system and the new in a manner which indicates a sincere desire to promote interreligious harmony.

- A greater concern with living out their new faith personally. If others are attracted to their lifestyle or show interest in any way, they are willing to discuss the faith, but only in a low-key fashion.

The Islam of the "liberals" is far more tolerant of other religious faiths, even freely borrowing from them and actively advocating interreligious dialogue. Their Islam is less critical of Western civilization, and consequently far more assimilationist with regard to American culture. It accords women greater equality with regard to societal—including political—roles than traditional Islamic cultures, and it views critically what has passed for "Islam" in the countries of the Muslim heartland. It renounces the superior air which has characterized most Muslim conservatives and instead adopts a more thoughtful and self-critical attitude. Currently it appears that this form of Islam is winning the day in America.

What Kind of Influence Will Islam Have?

Concerning the influence that converts to Islam have on American society as a whole, one can speak of two large-scale effects.

First, as an increasing number of non-African-Americans convert to Islam and tell of their experiences, it is likely that the religion's perception by the American public will undergo a subtle transformation. Currently, the stereotype of Muslims includes the Middle Eastern "ethnic" and the African-American who has joined Louis Farrakhan's Nation of Islam or Warith Deen Muhammad's Sunni organization. But increasingly European names and faces appear in the literature used to publicize the religion. Ethnic Muslims desire to place such persons in the spotlight in order to produce a different image of Islam.

The transformation will be slow, however. Currently, comparatively few Anglos have converted, and many of these are reluctant to have their conversion experiences publicized due to the negative social image connected with Islam. But some, like Jeffrey Lang, are willing to experience possible misunderstandings and ostracism. They hope that others will take courage from such examples, and that conversion to Islam by Anglo-Americans will become socially accepted.

This fact has particular significance for America's evangelical Christians. They have been the global frontrunners in religious proselytization for at least three centuries. But after several decades of "warming up," Islam is now coming into its stride, and Christians are beginning to watch with anxiety as Muslims close the gap. Some predict that the adherents of Islam globally will come to outnumber Christians in the next century. These predictions have led to the development of an Islamic focus for several missionary sending agencies.

In addition, conferences, seminars and educational training programs have been designed to discuss and to devise ways of forestalling the Muslim advance. The evangelistic focus on peoples living within the "10-40 Window"—between the tenth and fortieth lines of latitude north of the equator—includes virtually every Muslim country.

The situation, however, will most likely turn out to be much more complex than simple competition between Muslims and Christians for the "souls" of men and women. As Muslims learn of their increased profile as "targets" of Christian missionaries,[2] they will develop defensive measures. At the same time, they will step up their own proselytization activity and become increasingly "evangelical" with the religion of Islam. Their intent, of course, will be to increase conversions away from Christianity and toward Islam.

What may happen, however, is a reversal of what occurred during the nineteenth century. Then Christian missionaries arrived in the Muslim world and began to preach that due to their rejection of the biblical claims regarding Jesus, all Muslims would suffer eternal punishment in hell. A relatively small number of conversions to Christianity occurred. Much more significant, however, was the resulting "revival" of Islam throughout the Middle East. Muslims, insulted by what they considered to be the arrogance of Western missionary personnel, turned to their *imams* and Qur'ans for answers to the Christians' claims. As a result, many Muslims became even more firmly entrenched in Islam.

It is not difficult to imagine a similar scenario unfolding in North America and Europe. As Muslims become increasingly vocal and seek to elicit conversions away from the Christian and Jewish communities, the latter two groups will be forced to re-examine their own traditions and may well renew their commitments to their faith systems. The Muslims will then have produced a "revival" and entrenchment of the West's most influential religious groups—precisely the opposite of what they intend.

Thus there is no need for evangelicals to speak of Muslims as "Christianity's most dangerous enemy," as if Christians will be forced to fight a courageous battle that is ultimately doomed to failure. Instead we must continue with the Commission we have been given: to preach the gospel to all of creation and to make disciples among all peoples. It may well be that true Christianity will become a minority religion compared to the number of Muslims—indeed, this author would maintain that this is already the case, and has actually always been so. But being a minority should not give us pause.

And if in the midst of our communication of the gospel only a few Muslims convert to Christianity, this should not surprise us. For Jesus told us plainly that the road that leads to life is narrow, and only a few find it (Matthew 7:13-14; Luke 13:23-27). He informed His original disciples of this fact—and then ordered them to preach the gospel to every human being anyway. We now stand in the place of those disciples, and we must be no less faithful to the mission than they.

Lest the above paragraph be interpreted as too pessimistic or defeatist, let me add that the Bible also gives us specific promises regarding our expectations for success in this mission. Paul exhorts the Galatians not to become weary in doing good deeds (6:9). Let us take this directive to heart. Let us resolve to do good to the Muslims that we meet, helping them to adapt and adjust to American culture, aiding them in learning our worldview, customs and language. In the process of teaching and serving them, we can do what will ultimately prove to be the greatest good we can possibly perform for them: sharing the good news of salvation available to them as a free gift from the One True God.

Notes

1 See Jeffrey Lang, *Struggling to Surrender* (Beltsville, MD: Amana Pub., 1994) and Carol Anway, *Daughters of Another Path* (Lee's Summit, MO: YAWNA Pub., 1995).

2 See, for instance, Nahid Khan, "Zwimming for Muslim Souls: The Samuel Zwemer Institute for Muslim Studies," *Islamic Horizons,* April 1989, 23ff.

Appendix

Resources for Muslim Ministry

Following is a list of organizations which provide books, booklets, tracts and audio-visual materials to use in witnessing to Muslims.

Anis Shorrosh Evangelistic Association, P.O. Box 577, Spanish Fort, AL 36527; (205) 621-0507. Books, booklets.

American Bible Society, 1865 Broadway, New York, NY 10023; (212) 408-1200; Fax: (212) 408-1512. Bibles, Bible portions in various languages.

Arabic Communication Center, P.O. Box 60498, Pasadena, CA 91106.

Audio Scriptures International, P.O. Box 28417, San Diego, CA 92198-8417; (619) 673-0867. Bible and other taped messages in Arabic, Urdu, etc.

The Bible League, 16801 Van Dam Road, South Holland, IL 60473; (708) 331-2094; Fax: (708) 331-7172. Booklets (multiple languages): *Sharing the Good News with Muslims, The Prophets and the Word;* Gospel portions.

Blessed Hope Ministry, P.O. Box 2581, Springfield, VA 22152; (703) 451-6180; Fax: (703) 451-2283. Books: *La Ellaha Ella Allah, The Legend of Kaaba, Jinn in the Bible and the Quran, Muhammad and Christ.* Debates.

Caleb Project, 10 W. Dry Creek Circle, Littleton, CO 80120; (303) 730-4170; Fax: (303) 730-4177; info@cproject.com. Manual: *Exploring the Land: A Manual for Researching Unreached Peoples.*

Center for Ministry to Muslims, 2032 East Kearney, Suite 205, Springfield, MO 65803. Booklets, tracts.

Center for Ministry to Muslims, 1315 Portland Ave., Minneapolis, MN 55404.

Christian Duplications International, 1710 Lee Road, Orlando, FL 32810; (800) 327-9332; Fax: (407) 578-1880. The Bible on tape in Arabic, Urdu, etc.

Christian Information Network, 11025 State Highway 83, Colorado Springs, CO 80921; (719) 522-1040; Fax: (719) 548-9000.

Fellowship of Faith for Muslims, 205 Yonge St., Rm. 25, Toronto, Ontario M5B 1N2, Canada; (416) 364-5054. Tracts, prayer guides, booklets.

Fellowship of Isa, 4601 Excelsior Blvd., Suite 301, Minneapolis, MN 55416; (612) 933-6236.

Good News for the Crescent World, P.O. Box 13214, Arlington, TX 76014; (817) 275-3413.

Good Shepherd Ministries, P.O. Box 40248, Pasadena, CA 91114; (818) 398-2495. Books, tracts, booklets. Catalog of books, booklets, Bible portions, etc.

Goodwill Studies, P.O. Box 10671, Gladstone, MO 64118.

Horizons International, Box 18478, Boulder, CO 80308-1478; (303) 442-3333. Book and tape catalog; tracts.

International Institute for the Study of Islam and Christianity, P.O. Box 16474, Washington, DC 20041; (540) 338-7909; Fax: (540) 338-5924. In England: IISIC, St. Andrew's Centre, St. Andrew's Road, Plaistow, London, E13 8QD UK; 0171-474 0743; Fax: 0171-511 4874. Bi-monthly periodical: *I.I.S.I.C. Bulletin.*

International Outreach, Inc., P.O. Box 40130, Pasadena, CA 91114. Tracts, booklets.

Iranian Christians International, Inc., P.O. Box 25607, Colorado Springs, CO 80936; (719) 596-0010; Fax: (719) 574-1141. Regional discipleship and training conferences; publisher of *Mojdeh* (magazine). Bookstore, materials in Persian, Dari, Pushtu and English.

Mandate Press, P.O. Box 40129, Pasadena, CA 91114.

MARC Publications, 919 West Huntington Drive, Monrovia, CA 91016.

Ministries to Muslims, 4352 Austin Bluffs Parkway, #357, Colorado Springs, CO 80918; (719) 597-0609. Booklets, videos, etc.

Multi-Language Media, Box 301, Ephrata, PA 17522; (717) 738-0582. Bibles in eighty languages, *Resources for Understanding Muslims.*

Noor ul Haq (Light of Truth), P.O. Box 583279, Minneapolis, MN 55458.

Al-Nour, P.O. Box 985, Colorado Springs, CO 80901. Booklets, tracts.

The Pen Versus the Sword, P.O. Box 661336, Los Angeles, CA 90066. Booklets.

People of the Book, 1731 West Berwyn Ave., Chicago, IL 60640; (312) 784-6221. Books, booklets, audiovisuals.

Radio Bible Class, 3000 Kraft SE., Grand Rapids, MI 49555.

Saatu'l Islah, The Back to God Hour, 6555 W. College Dr., Palos Heights, IL 60463; (708) 371-8700.

Thirty Days Muslim Prayer Focus International, P.O. Box 188, Ashgrove QLD.4060, Australia; Fax: 61-7-3663111. USA affiliate: P.O. Box 26479, Colorado Springs, CO 80936-6479; (719) 442-6409; Fax: (719) 380-0936.

Vision 3 Productions, 19721 64th Ave. W., Suite 7, Lynnwood, WA 98036. VHS video series: *The Real Story: A Christian's Guide to the Middle East.*

Voice of Truth, P.O. Box 15013, Colorado Springs, CO 80935; (719) 574-5900; Fax: (719) 574-6075. Books, cassettes, etc.

The Way Publications, P.O. Box 42085, Los Angeles, CA 90042.

WorldChristian News & Books, P.O. Box 26479, Colorado Springs, CO 80936; (719) 442-6409; Fax: (719) 380-0936; e-mail: wcn@xc.org.

Glossary

ahl al-dhimma/dhimmi—literally "people of protection"/a "protected person." A special status given by Muslims to monotheistic religious groups (i.e., Christians and Jews) which allowed these groups to retain their places and customs of worship.

ahl al-kitab—literally "people of the Book." A special name given by Islam to the three major religions which have the Word of God (Scriptures) as the foundation for their belief and practice. The people of the Book are thus Jews, Christians and Muslims.

al-Janna—"the garden." The Muslim name for paradise or "heaven," by which is meant the abode of the righteous for eternity.

ayatollah—"the eye of Allah." A term designating the chief leaders of the Shi'ite Muslim faith today. This would be a status roughly equivalent to that of a cardinal or an archbishop within Christianity.

baraka—"blessing." The special spiritual power which folk Muslims believe that their leaders possess, a power which can be used to bring blessings to a community or individuals.

caliph—the chief leader of Islam, from a word which means "representative," implying that the *caliph* was the representative of both Allah and Muhammad. Roughly equivalent to the position of the Christian Pope, the *caliphate* was ended in 1924.

da'i—"one who invites." The Arabic term for "missionary."

dar al-Islam; dar al-harb—"abode of Islam; abode of war." Designations given by Muslims to geographical territories throughout the earth. The *dar al-Islam* is any location where the Muslim Shari'a (law) is the law of the land. The *dar al-harb* is the opposite—any location where the Muslim law does not reign supreme.

da'wah—"an invitation." The Arabic term for "missionary activity."

din al-fitr—"the religion of nature." Muslims believe that all humans are born Muslims, and are "corrupted" and "led astray" to other religions by their parents and environment.

Eid al-Adha/Eid al-Fitr—the two major Muslim holidays. *Eid al-Adha* is the celebration which closes the season of *hajj,* or pilgrimage; and *Eid al-Fitr* closes the month of Ramadan.

hadith—"tradition." The collection of traditions regarding the life, sayings and deeds of Muhammad.

hajj—"pilgrimage." The pilgrimage made to Mecca by Muslims at least once in their lives.

halal—"permitted." The term used by Muslims to designate food (and on occasion other items) which is in accordance with Islamic law.

IIIT—International Institute for Islamic Thought, a Muslim "think tank" located in Herndon, a Northern Virginia suburb of Washington, D.C.

Ikhwan al-Muslimun—"the Muslim Brotherhood." An Egyptian Muslim organization founded and led by Hasan al-Banna, introducing a new missionary strategy for Muslims to use in reaching non-Muslims.

imam—"prayer leader." A Muslim leader who was originally the leader of the daily prayers and caretaker of a mosque. Currently the *imam* is becoming more and more the equivalent of a Protestant pastor with respect to the functions he fulfills.

injil—"the Evangelium." Arabic word for "the Gospels," by which is meant the Christian New Testament.

islamization—the process by which the institutions of a nation are transformed into Muslim institutions.

Jama'at i-Islami—"the Islamic Society." A Pakistani Muslim organization founded and led by Abul Ala Mawdudi, introducing a new missionary strategy for Muslims to use in reaching non-Muslims.

jihad—"struggle, effort, exertion." The term used to describe the Muslim world's efforts to spread the gospel of Islam and the kingdom of Islam over the entire earth, accomplishing submission ("islam") of all human beings to Allah.

jizya—a tax imposed by Muslims upon all *dhimmis* (protected persons) in return for military protection.

Ka'ba—the cube-shaped shrine located in Mecca which is the chief destination for the Muslim *hajj* (pilgrimage). Muslims believe that it was originally built by Abraham and Ishmael. At the time of Muhammad, it was a temple housing pagan deities of the pre-Islamic Arabs.

mamluks—"owned ones." Slaves owned by Egyptian Muslims which during the Middle Ages became a ruling class themselves.

marabout—a North African Muslim leader endowed with *baraka*.

masjid—the Arabic word which appears in English as the word "mosque." It is also the specific designation by African-American Muslims for their places of worship (i.e., a "Masjid Muhammad").

mujaddid—"a renewer." A Muslim who brings about reform or revival within the Muslim community. Muslims believe that such a person has appeared every 100 years since the death of Muhammad.

mujahid—"one who performs *jihad.*" Literally, this is one who "exerts effort," but the term is most often used today to designate "soldiers of God."

OPEC—the Organization of Petroleum Exporting Countries; a multinational corporation of (mainly) Muslim states which seek to control the production and pricing of crude oil.

Ramadan—the month of fasting, observed by all devout Muslims once each year.

rasul—"apostle; messenger." A prophet who is distinguished by having brought not only a message to mankind, but Scriptures as well. Thus Moses, Jesus and Muhammad all bear the title of *rasul.*

Shahada—"the testimony or the witness," the creed of all Muslims: "There is no God but Allah, and Muhammad is his messenger."

Shari'a—"the path." Arabic term usually translated "Muslim law" but which is actually a more comprehensive term designating all of the precepts one follows in order to be a Muslim.

shaykh—term designating a Muslim scholar, who is often elevated to leadership due to his great learning.

Shi'ite—one of two large divisions of Islam. Shi'ites are the minority group (approximately ten percent of world Islam) who believe that the successors of Muhammad should have been limited to his own personal family. Thus Ali, Muhammad's cousin and designated heir, should have been the first *caliph*.

Sirah—a biography of the life of Muhammad.

Sufi—term used to describe a Muslim who is devoted to mystical practices, seeking direct knowledge and experience of Allah.

Sunni—one of two large divisions of Islam. Sunnis are the majority group (approximately ninety percent of world Islam) who believe that the successors of Muhammad should have been elected democratically from among Muhammad's followers.

tariqa—a Sufi "school" which was usually built around the leadership and teaching of a single man. Eventually the *tariqas* became institutions akin to the Christian monasteries of Europe.

tawrah—"Torah." The Arabic term for the Pentateuch, but which by extension is applied to the entire Old Testament.

Select Bibliography of Muslim Ministry and Islam

The following books are recommended for learning more about Islam and ministry to Muslims.

Abdul-Haqq, Abdiyah Akbar. *Sharing Your Faith with a Muslim*. Minneapolis, MN: Bethany, 1980.

Barboza, Steven. *American Jihad: Islam after Malcolm X*. New York: Doubleday, 1994.

Burness, Margaret. *What Would You Say If . . . : Plays to Help Christian Witness to Muslim Women*. Ghana: Africa Christian, 1980.

Chapman, Colin. *Cross and Crescent: Responding to the Challenge of Islam*. Downers Grove, IL: InterVarsity Press, 1995.

Cooper, Anne, ed. *Ishmael My Brother: A Biblical Course on Islam.* London: Evangelical Missionary Alliance, 1985.

Cragg, Kenneth. *Muhammad and the Christian.* Maryknoll, NY: Orbis, 1984.

_____. *Jesus and the Muslim.* London: George Allen & Unwin, 1985.

Dretke, James P. *A Christian Approach to Muslims: Reflections from West Africa.* Pasadena, CA: William Carey Library, 1979.

Ellis, Carl. *Malcolm: The Man Behind the X.* Chattanooga, TN: Accord Publications, 1993.

_____. *Free at Last: The Gospel in the African-American Experience.* 2nd ed. Downers Grove, IL: InterVarsity Press, 1996.

Geisler, Norman L. and Abdul Saleeb. *Answering Islam: The Crescent in the Light of the Cross.* Grand Rapids, MI: Baker Book House, 1993.

Goldsmith, Martin. *Islam and Christian Witness.* Downers Grove, IL: InterVarsity Press, 1983.

Haddad, Yvonne Yazbeck. *The Muslims of America.* New York: Oxford University Press, 1991.

Haddad, Yvonne Yazbeck and Jane Idleman Smith. *Muslim Communities in North America.* New York: State University of New York Press, 1994.

_____. *Mission to America: Five Islamic Sectarian Communities in North America.* Gainesville, FL: University Press of Florida, 1993.

Haddad, Yvonne Yazbeck and Adair Lummis. *Islamic Values in the United States: A Comparative Study.* New York: Oxford University Press, 1987.

Haley, Alex. *The Autobiography of Malcolm X.* New York: Ballantine Books, 1965.

Hamada, Louis Bahjat. *God Loves the Arabs, Too.* Nashville, TN: Winston-Derek Publishers, 1986.

Hodgson, Marshall G.S. *The Venture of Islam.* 3 vols. Chicago: University of Chicago Press, 1974.

Kateregga, Badru and David Shenk. *Islam and Christianity: A Muslim and Christian in Dialogue.* Grand Rapids, MI: Eerdmans, 1981.

Lincoln, C. Eric. *The Black Muslims in America.* 3rd ed. Grand Rapids, MI: Eerdmans Publishing Co., 1994.

Livingstone, Greg. *Planting Churches in Muslim Cities: A Team Approach.* Grand Rapids, MI: Baker Book House, 1993.

Madany, Bassam M. *The Bible and Islam: Sharing God's Word with a Muslim.* Palos Heights, IL: The Back to God Hour, 1987.

Marsh, Charles R. *Share Your Faith with a Muslim.* Chicago: Moody Press, 1975.

Matheny, Tim. *Reaching the Arabs: A Felt Need Approach.* Pasadena, CA: William Carey Library, 1981.

McCloud, Aminah Beverly. *African American Islam.* New York: Routledge, 1995.

McCurry, Donald M., ed. *The Gospel and Islam: A 1978 Compendium.* Monrovia, CA: MARC, 1979.

McDowell, Josh and John Gilchrist. *The Islam Debate.* San Bernardino, CA: Here's Life Publishers, 1983.

The Meaning of the Holy Qur'an. 9th ed. Translated by Abdullah Yusef Ali. Beltsville, MD: AMANA Publications, 1998.

Miller, William. *A Christian Response to Islam.* Philadelphia: Presbyterian and Reformed Publishing Co., 1976.

_____. *Ten Muslims Meet Christ.* Grand Rapids, MI: Eerdmans, 1969. Reprint, 1987.

Musk, Bill. *The Unseen Face of Islam.* London: MARC, 1989.

Nasr, Seyyed Hossein. *A Young Muslim's Guide to the Modern World.* Chicago: Kazi Publications, 1994.

Nazir-Ali, Michael. *Islam: A Christian Perspective.* Exeter, England: Paternoster, 1983.

_____. *Frontiers in Muslim-Christian Encounter.* Oxford: Regnum, 1987.

Otis, George Jr. *The Last of the Giants: Lifting the Veil on Islam and the End Times.* Tarrytown, NY: Revell, 1991.

Parshall, Phil. *New Paths in Muslim Evangelism: Evangelical Approaches to Contextualization.* Grand Rapids, MI: Baker, 1980.

_____. *Bridges to Islam: A Christian Perspective on Folk Islam.* Grand Rapids, MI: Baker, 1983.

_____. *Beyond the Mosque: Christians within Muslim Community.* Grand Rapids, MI: Baker, 1985.

_____. *The Cross and the Crescent: Understanding the Muslim Mind and Heart.* Wheaton, IL: Tyndale, 1989.

_____. *Inside the Community: Understanding Muslims Through Their Traditions.* Grand Rapids, MI: Baker Book House, 1994.

Poston, Larry. *Islamic Da'wah in the West: Muslim Missionary Activity and the Dynamics of Conversion to Islam.* New York: Oxford University Press, 1992.

Rahman, Fazlur. *Islam* (Second Edition). Chicago: University of Chicago Press, 1979.

_____. *Major Themes of the Qur'an.* Chicago: Bibliotheca Islamica, 1980.

Saal, William J. *Reaching Muslims for Christ.* Chicago: Moody Press, 1991.

Schlorff, Samuel P., ed. *Discipleship in Islamic Society.* Upper Darby, PA: North Africa Mission, 1981.

Shorrosh, Anis. *Islam Revealed: A Christian Arab's View of Islam.* Nashville, TN: Thomas Nelson, 1988.

Voll, John Obert. *Islam: Continuity and Change in the Modern World.* Boulder, CO: Westview Press, 1982.

Watt, W. Montgomery. *Muslim-Christian Encounters: Perceptions and Misperceptions.* New York: Routledge, 1991.

Woodberry, Dudley. *Muslims and Christians on the Emmaus Road.* Monrovia, CA: MARC, 1989.